How to Start & Manage a Property Management Business

A Practical Way to Start Your Own Business

By
Jerre G. Lewis and Leslie D. Renn

How to Start & Manage a Property Management Business

Lewis & Renn Associates, Inc.
Business & Professional Publishing
10315 Harmony Drive
Interlochen, Michigan 49643
(231) 275-7287

Leslie D. Renn
President

Jerre G. Lewis
Secretary-Treasurer

ISBN # 1-57916-069-7
Library of Congress Catalog Card Number
99-094138

TABLE OF CONTENTS

Chapter 1

Introduction

Selecting the right Property Management business opportunity requires careful, thorough evaluations of yourself. Owning your own business is as much a part of the American dream as owning a home, and for you, this urge represents one of life's most exciting challenges. This book is for those men and women who someday may go into business for themselves and for those who are already in business for themselves but wish to strengthen their entrepreneurial and managerial skills.

Entrepreneurs come in all shapes and sizes, personalities, and lifestyles. They are usually highly motivated, hard-working individuals who receive satisfaction from taking risks. Your business should interest you, not just be an income generator. Analyze your personal style. Do you like working with people? Are you a self starter, goal oriented, persistent, a risk taker, willing to work hard and long hours?

If you have been honest in evaluating yourself, you will now select the right type of business. Before you can determine which of the multitude of businesses is right for you to start, you must evaluate the businesses you want to start by asking these questions. Is the business area growing? How does the economy affect it? Who dominates its market? Once you have considered a business that satisfies your needs and interest you must prepare a formal business plan by following the outline given in this book.

Small businesses constitute a dynamic and critical sector of the U.S. economy. Every year in the United States more than 600,000 new businesses are launched by independent men and women eager to make their own decisions, express their own ideas, and be their own bosses. But running your own business is not as easy as it may seem. There can be problems with the inventory, or getting the right goods delivered on time. Yet, managing one's own business can be a personally and financially rewarding experience for an individual strong enough to meet the test. A person with stamina, maturity, and creativity, one who is willing to make sacrifices, may find making a go of a struggling enterprise an exhilarating challenge with many compensations.

Small business owners are a dedicated group of people who work hard and whose hours on the job usually exceed the nine-to-five routine. The owner's commitment is the key to many successful small businesses; an entrepreneur is able to communicate ideas, lead, plan, be patient, and work well with people.

Managing a business requires more than the possession of technical knowledge. Because most small businesses are started by technical people, such as engineers and salesmen, their managerial acumen is often less developed than their technical skills. The need to plan for management is common to every type of and size of business, and there are certain steps that must be taken. Although some of them are very elementary — such as applying for a city business permit — the most important are often complex and difficult and require the advice of specialists: accountants, attorneys, insurance brokers, and/or bankers. For almost any business though, the first step will be to translate the entrepreneur's basic idea into a concrete plan for action.

To gauge your level of entrepreneurial spirit, the following quiz was created. Please answer each question honestly and then total the columns.

ENTREPRENEURIAL QUIZ

	YES	NO	SOMETIMES
1. I am a self-starter. Nobody has to tell me how to get going.	___	___	___
2. I am capable of getting along with just about everybody.	___	___	___
3. I have no trouble getting people to follow my lead.	___	___	___
4. I like to be in charge of things and see them through.	___	___	___
5. I always plan ahead before beginning a project. I am usually the one who gets everyone organized.	___	___	___
6. I have a lot of stamina. I can keep going as long as necessary.	___	___	___
7. I have no trouble making decisions and can make up my mind in a hurry.	___	___	___
8. I say exactly what I mean. People can trust me.	___	___	___
9. Once I make my mind up to do something, nothing can stop me.	___	___	___
10. I am in excellent health and have a lot of energy.	___	___	___

	YES	NO	SOMETIMES

11. I have experience or technical knowledge in the business I intend to start.

     _____   _____   _____

12. I feel comfortable taking risks if it is something I really believe in.

     _____   _____   _____

13. I have good communication skills.

     _____   _____   _____

14. I am flexible in my dealings with people and situations.

     _____   _____   _____

15. I consider myself creative and resourceful.

     _____   _____   _____

16. I can analyze a situation and take steps to correct problems.

     _____   _____   _____

17. I think I am capable of maintaining a good working relationship with employees.

     _____   _____   _____

18. I am not a dictator. I am willing to listen to employees, customers and suppliers.

     _____   _____   _____

19. I am not rigid in my policies. I am willing to adjust to meet the needs of employees, customers, and suppliers.

     _____   _____   _____

20. More than anything else, I want to run my own business.

     _____   _____   _____

Total of Column #1 _____

Total of Column #2 _____

Total of Column #3 _____

If the total of Column #1 is the highest, then you will probably be very successful in running your own business.

If the total of Column #2 is the highest, you may find that running a business is more than you can handle.

If the total of Column #3 is the highest, you should consider taking on a partner who is strong in your weak areas.

NOTE: This quiz was adapted from the Small Business Administration publication *Checklist for Going Into Business*.

Notes

Chapter 2

Planning the Business

The Dream of self-employment can be fulfilled. You don't need to finance the opening of an elaborate office or facility to start your own one-person corporation either. You can start your own Property Management business.

Anyone preparing to run an Property Management business needs to learn a great deal to assure the best possible chance for success.

GETTING STARTED

The following is a list of what you need to accomplish to insure that your Property Management endeavor will head in the right direction.

1. Define your educational background and work experience.

2. Survey all the basic types of Property Management businesses.

3. Define what products or services your Property Management business will be marketing.

4. Define who will be using your products/services.

5. Define why they will be purchasing your products/services.

6. List all competitors in your Property Management marketing area.

ZONING REGISTRATIONS

Property Management businesses are subject to many laws and regulations enforced by state, county, township governmental units. Most jurisdictions now have codes, a zoning board, and an appeal board which regulate businesses. Areas often are zoned residential, commercial or industrial.

You must become familiar with these regulations. If you are doing business in violation of these regulations, you could be issued a cease and desist order or fined.

Certain kinds of goods cannot be produced in the home, though these restrictions vary somewhat from state-to-state. Most states outlaw home production of fireworks, drugs, poisons, explosives, sanitary/medical products and some toys.

Many localities have registration requirements for new businesses. You will need to obtain a work certificate or license from the state.

TAX REQUIREMENTS

<u>Application for Employer Identification Number</u>, Form SS-4. This registers you with the Internal Revenue Service as a business. If you have employees, you should ask for Circular E along with your ID number. Circular E explains federal income and social security tax withholding requirements.

<u>Employer's Annual Unemployment Tax Return</u>, Form 940. This is only if you have employees. It's used to report and pay the Federal Unemployment Compensation Tax.

<u>Employee's Withholding Allowance Certificate</u>, W-4. Every employee must complete the W-4 so the proper amount of income tax can be withheld from the

employee's pay. If the employee claims more than 15 allowances or a complete withholding exemption while having a salary of more than $200 a week, a copy of the W-4 must go to the IRS.

Employer's Wage and Tax Statement, W-2. Used to report to the IRS the total taxes withheld and total compensation paid to each employee per year.

Reconciliation/Transmittal of Income and Tax Statements, W-3. Used to total all information from the W-2. Sent to the Social Security Administration.

The IRS puts on monthly workshops on understanding and using these forms. Call your local IRS office for further information.

States also have various tax form requirements including: an unemployment tax form, a certificate of registration application, a sales and use tax return, an employer's quarterly contribution and payroll report, an income tax withholding registration form, an income tax withholding form, and others. Some forms apply only to employers who have employees. Your local IRS office and state Office of Taxation can provide you with listings of forms you will need to start your business. The following table outlines Federal tax form requirements.

Every small business begins with an idea — a product to be manufactured or sold, a service to be performed.

Whatever the business or its degree of complexity, the owner needs a business plan in order to transform a vision into a working operation.

This business plan should describe in writing and in figures the proposed Property Management business and its products, services, or manufacturing processes. It should also include an analysis of the market, a marketing strategy, an organizational plan, and measurable financial objectives.

WHAT SHOULD A BUSINESS PLAN COVER?

It should be a thorough and objective analysis of both personal abilities and business requirements for a particular product or service. It should define strategies for such functions as marketing and production, organization and legal aspects, accounting and finance. A business plan should answer such questions as:

What do I want and what am I capable of doing?

What are the most workable ways of achieving my goals?

What can I expect in the future?

There is no single best way to begin. What follows is simply a guide and can be changed to suit individual needs.

1. Define Long-term goals.
2. State short-term.
3. Set marketing strategies to meet goals and objectives.
4. Analyze available resources.
5. Assemble financial data.
6. Review plan.

Please refer to Figure 2.1 for a complete business plan outline.

The business operator with a realistic plan has the best chance for success.

Figure 2.1

BUSINESS PLAN FOR SMALL BUSINESSES

I. Type of Business

II. Location

III. Target Market

IV. Planning Process

V. Organizational Structure

VI. Staffing Procedures

VII. Market Strategy

IX. Financial Planning

X. Budgeted Balance Sheet

XI. Budgeted Income Statement

XII. Budgeted Cash Flow Statement

XIII. Break-Even Chart

*Notes*_____

Chapter 3

Marketing Strategies
for an Property Management Business

As a potential Property Management business owner, it is important to learn all you can about marketing. You will need to know how to identify your market and how to market your product or service.

As a business person who looks for a profit from the sale of goods, you recognize that without people who want to buy, there is no demand for the things you want to sell. Thus, it is important that, in addition to knowing about the functions of marketing, you also study the activities that will influence the consumer. When you satisfy the specific needs and wants of the customer, then he or she may be willing to pay you a price that will include a profit for you — and to make a profit is one of the reasons you have become an Property Management business owner. Although there are many activities connected with marketing, most of them can be classified in these categories: buy, finance, transport, standardize, store, insure, advertise and sell.

Target Market Analysis

Before you can create a successful marketing campaign, it's necessary to determine your target market (toward whom to direct your energies). The whole concept of target marketing can seem very scary at first. On the surface, targeting appears to be limiting the scope of the pool of potential customers. Many people fear that by defining a market, they will lose business. They are concerned that they will choose the wrong market. Or that other practitioners will take just anybody and therefore some of their business.

You must keep in mind that the purpose of defining your target market is to make your life easier and increase the productivity of your promotional endeavors. Many opportunities exist in this world and it's impossible to pursue them all or be everything to everyone. You need to know where to focus your energy and money when it comes to promotion and advertising.

The two most common means of market analysis are demographics and psychographics, which describe a person in terms of objective data and personality attributes.

Demographics are statistics such as:
- age
- gender
- income level
- geographic location
- occupation
- education level

Psychographics are lifestyle factors including:
- special interest activities
- philosophical beliefs
- social factors
- cultural involvements

The more you know about your potential customers, the easier it is to develop an appropriate position statement and design an effective marketing campaign. The actual number of target markets you have depends mainly upon the size of your practice and the scope of your knowledge.

Your Target Market Profile

In order to clarify your target market(s) you need to delineate the demographic and psychographic factors and then identify the characteristics your customers have in common.

Describe your current customers and those who are most likely your future customers:

What is the age range and average age of your customers?

What is the percentage of males?

What is the percentage of females?

What is the average educational level of your customers?

Where do your customers live?

What are the occupations of your customers?

Where do your customers work?

What is the average annual income level of your customers?

Of what special interest groups are your customers members?

What is the primary reason your customers use your services?

Defining Your Target Market(s)

Write a descriptive statement for each of your target markets (refer to your "Target Market Profile"). Include a brief overview of the services you are providing to that group and a detailed analysis of the characteristics of the specific clientele.

Target Market 1:

Target Market 2:

Target Market 3:

Property Management Business Marketing

The foundation for creating a thriving customer base.

A. Overview

This section is about clarifying your beliefs and attitudes toward your profession and determining the image you wish to portray.

1. Describe the "character" that you want for your business. Depict the image you want to convey:

2. State your philosophy in regard to your business:

3. Describe your philosophy regarding your practice in business:

B. Customer Profile

This is a descriptive analysis of your current and potential customers — who they are, what their interests are, and where you can find them. Include each of your target markets.

1. Target Market 1:

2. Target Market 2:

3. Target Market 3:

C. Competition's Marketing Assessment

The first phase in planning your promotional campaign is appraising the competition. List each of your major competitors and describe the marketing strategies they utilize. Be certain to include where and how often they advertise.

1. Major Competitor 1:

2. Major Competitor 2:

3. Major Competitor 3:

4. Major Competitor 4:

5. Major Competitor 5:

6. Major Competitor 6:

Property Management Marketing Planning

Outline for Marketing:

I. Produce/Service Concept
   A. Name of produce or service
   B. Descriptive characteristics of product or service
   C. Unit sales
   D. Analysis of market trends

II. Number of Customers in Market Area:
   A. Profile of customers
   B. Average customer expenditure
   C. Total market

III. Your Market Potential:
   A. Total market divided by competition
   B. Total market multiplied by percent who will buy your product

IV. Needs of Customers:
   A. Identification
   B. Pleasure
   C. Social approval
   D. Personal interest
   E. Price

V. Direct Marketing Sources:
   A. Trade magazines
   B. Trade associates
   C. Small Business Administration (SBA)
   D. Government publications
   E. Yellow Pages
   F. Marketing directories

VI. Customer Profile:
   A. Geographical
   B. Gender
   C. Age range
   D. Income brackets
   E. Occupation
   F. Educational level

Chapter 4

Promoting the Property Management Business

When a new business is opened, the owner must be prepared to publicize the business or its chance for success will be slim. Only a few businesses — such as those with a prime location, nationally known name, or a built-in clientele — can succeed without advertising to promote market awareness and stimulate sales.

The first purpose — promoting customer awareness — applies as much to established businesses as to newcomers.

In the Property Management business, you will find it easier to retain old customers than to win new ones. When old customers move away from your area, or when their buying needs change, you need new customers to maintain your sales volume. If you expect your business to gain, you will need additional new customers. New customers are those who move into your area or who have grown into your line of products because now they can afford them or they need them. We see advertising and we hear advertising all around us, and yet that is only a part of it. Through advertising, you call the attention of customers to your products.

As a small business owner, you may advertise your business through your location. People pass by and are attracted to your operation because of what you are selling. To get a better idea of what advertising is, consider some of the following functions of advertising:

1. *To inform:* Letting customers know what you have for sale through brochures, leaflets, newspapers, radio, TV, and etc.

2. *Persuade:* Persuasion is the art of leading individuals to do what you want them to do. There are sales personnel who have persuasive sales presentations, but persuasion in advertising is nonpersonal. The appeal is made through the printed or spoken words or a picture. The influence of an ad on readers occurs as purchasers choose what they want among different products, and different wants. To gain the actions you want — a sale — you must persuade a customer to examine personally what you have for sale.

3. *Reminder:* Advertising performs it's third function when it reminds those who have been persuaded to buy once that the same product will bring satisfaction. The ad will also remind a customer of the characteristics of a product purchased some time ago, and where he or she bought it. Because customers change their loyalty to a place of business, their taste for products, and often their trading area patronage, advertising is necessary to draw new customers and to hold old customers. To generate results from advertising that will be profitable to your business, you will have to produce answers to the what, where and how of advertising.

What to Advertise

The nature of your business will partially answer the question "Shall I advertise goods or services?" What are the outstanding features of your business? Is it unique in any way? Does it have strong points? Do you have something to offer that the competition is not able to duplicate? Answers to these questions will give you a start in deciding what to advertise.

Where to Advertise

Of course, you will want to advertise within your marketing area, however there are a few guidelines to remember:

A. Who are your customers?

B. What is their income range?

C. Why do they buy?

D. How do they buy? Do they pay Cash? Charge?

E. What is the radius of your market area?

How to Advertise:

In determining how to advertise, you will have to consider your dollar allocation for advertising and the media suitable to your particular kind of business. However, it is important to have a balance between the presentation of the product or service being advertised and the application of three basic principles.

1. Gain the attention of the audience.

2. Establish a need.

3. Tell where that need may be filled.

See Figure A for an outline of the different advertising media and Figure B for budget on media goals.

Advertising Media

Media	Market Coverage	Type of Audience
Daily Newspaper	Single community or entire metro area; zoned editions sometimes available	General
Weekly Newspaper	Single community	Residents
Telephone Directory	Geographical area or occupational field served by the directory	Active shoppers for goods or services
Direct mail audience	Controlled by the advertiser	Controlled
Radio audience	Definable market area	Selected
Television audience	Definable market area	Various
Outdoor	Entire metro area	General auto drivers
Magazine	Entire metro area or magazine region	Selected audience

Figure A

Promotion and Advertising Plan — Property Management Business

In designing your promotional plan, it's wise to use a variety of media. You must have specific goals, time lines and budgets for each marketing application

Media	Goal	Timeline	Budget

Notes _____

Chapter 5

Financial Planning for an
Property Management Business

Financial planning is the process of analyzing and monitoring the financial performance of your business so you can assess your current position and anticipate future problem areas. The daily, monthly, seasonal, and yearly operation of your business requires attention to the figures that tell you about the firm's financial health.

Maintaining good financial records is a necessary part of doing business.

The increasing number of governmental regulations alone makes it virtually impossible to avoid keeping detailed records. Just as important is to keep them for yourself. The success of your business depends on them. An efficient system of record keeping can help you to:

- make management decisions
- compete in the marketplace
- monitor performance
- keep track of expenses
- eliminate unprofitable merchandise
- protect your assets
- prepare your financial statements

Financial skills should include understanding of the balance sheet, the profit-and-loss statement, cash flow projection, break-even analysis, and source and application of funds. In many businesses, the husband and wife run the business; it is especially important that both of them understand financial management. Most small business owners are not accountants, but they must understand the tool of financial management if they are going to be able to measure the return on their investment. Although good records are essential to good financial planning, they alone are not enough because their full use requires interpretation and analysis. The owner/manager's financial decisions concerning return on invested funds, approaches to banks, securing greater supplier credit, raising additional equity capital and so forth, can be more successful if he takes the time to develop understanding and use of the balance sheet and profit-and-loss statement.

Balance Sheet:

The balance sheet, Figure I, shows the financial condition of a business at the end of business on a specific day. It is called a balance sheet because the total assets balance with, or are equal to, total liabilities plus owner's capital balance. Current assets are those that the owner does not anticipate holding for long. This category includes cash, finished goods in inventory, and accounts receivable. Fixed assets are long-term assets, including plant and equipment. A third possible category is the intangible asset of goodwill. Liabilities are debts owed by the business, including both accounts payable, which are usually short-term, and notes payable, which are usually long-term debts such as mortgage payments. The difference between the value of the assets and the value of the liabilities is the capital. This category includes funds invested by the owner plus accumulated profits, less withdrawals.

The Income Statement:

This statement, Figure II, is also known as a profit-and loss (P&L) statement. It shows how a business has performed over a certain period of time. An income statement specifies sales, costs of sales, gross profit, expenses and net income or loss from operations.

Figure I

Financial Forecast

Opening Balance Sheet - Date

ASSETS

Current Assets

Cash and bank accounts		$
Accounts receivable		$
Inventory		$
Other current assets		$
TOTAL CURRENT ASSETS	(A)	$

Fixed Assets

Property owned		$
Furniture and equipment		$
Business automobile		$
Leasehold improvements		$
Other fixed assets		$
TOTAL FIXED ASSETS	(B)	$
TOTAL ASSETS	(A+B = X)	$

LIABILITIES

Current Liabilities (due within the next 12 months)

Bank loans		$
Other loans		$
Accounts payable		$
Other current liabilities		$
TOTAL CURRENT LIABILITIES	(C)	$

Long-term Liabilities

Mortgages		$
Long-term loans		$
Other long-term liabilities		$
TOTAL LONG-TERM LIABILITIES	(D)	$
TOTAL LIABILITIES	(C+D = Y)	$
NET WORTH	(X-Y = Z)	$
TOTAL NET WORTH AND LIABILITIES	(Y+Z)	$

Figure II

Business Income and Expense Forecast for the Next 12 Months

One year estimate ending _____, 19 _____

Projected Number of Clients

For your services _____

For your products _____

TOTAL NUMBER OF CLIENTS _____

Projected Income

Sessions $ _____

Product sales $ _____

Other $ _____

TOTAL INCOME $ _____

Projected Expenses

Start-up costs $ _____

Monthly expenses (x 12) $ _____

Annual expenses $ _____

TOTAL EXPENSES $ _____

TOTAL OPERATING PROFIT (OR LOSS) $ _____

CAPITAL REQUIRED FOR THE NEXT 12 MONTHS $ _____

27

Property Management Business

Start-Up Costs Worksheet	
Item	**Estimated Expense**
Open checking account	$
Telephone installation	$
Equipment	$
First & last month's rent, security deposit, etc.	$
Supplies	$
Business cards, stationery, etc.	$
Advertising and promotion package	$
Decorating and remodeling	$
Furniture and fixtures	$
Legal and professional fees	$
Insurance	$
Utility deposits	$
Beginning inventory	$
Installation of fixtures and equipment	$
Licenses and permits	$
Other	$
TOTAL	$

Fixed Annual Expense Worksheet	
Item	**Estimated Expense**
Property insurance	$
Business auto insurance	$
Licenses and permits	$
Liability insurance	$
Disability insurance	$
Professional society membership	$
Fees (legal, accounting, etc.)	$
Taxes	$
Other	$
TOTAL	$

Monthly Business Expense Worksheet		
Expense	**Estimated Monthly Cost**	**X 12**
Rent	$	$
Utilities	$	$
Telephone	$	$
Bank fees	$	$
Supplies	$	$
Stationery and business cards	$	$
Networking club dues	$	$
Education (seminars, books professional journals, etc.)	$	$
Business car (Payments, gas, repairs, etc)	$	$
Advertising and promotion	$	$
Postage	$	$
Entertainment	$	$
Repair, cleaning and maintenance	$	$
Travel	$	$
Business loan payments	$	$
Salary/Draw	$	$
Staff salaries	$	$
Miscellaneous	$	$
Taxes	$	$
Professional fees	$	$
Decorations	$	$
Furniture and fixtures	$	$
Equipment	$	$
Inventory	$	$
Other	$	$
TOTAL MONTHLY	$	$
TOTAL YEARLY		$

Cash Flow Forecast						
	January Estimate	January Actual	February Estimate	February Actual	March Estimate	March Actual
Beginning cash						
Plus monthly income from: Fees						
Sales						
Loans						
Other						
TOTAL CASH AND INCOME						
Expenses:						
Rent						
Utilities						
Telephone						
Bank fees						
Supplies						
Stationery and business cards						
Insurance						
Dues						
Education						
Auto						
Advertising and promotion						
Postage						
Entertainment						

Cash Flow Forecast (Continued)						
	January Estimate	January Actual	February Estimate	February Actual	March Estimate	March Actual
Repair and maintenance						
Travel						
Business loan payments						
Licenses and permits						
Salary/Draw						
Staff salaries						
Taxes						
Professional fees						
Decorations						
Furniture and fixtures						
Equipment						
Inventory						
Other Expenses						
TOTAL EXPENSES						
ENDING CASH (+/-)						

Notes _____

Chapter 6

Property Management Business Planning

Introduction

Our increasingly service oriented economy offers a widening spectrum of opportunities for customized and personalized small business growth. Though untrained entrepreneurs have traditionally had a high rate of failure, small businesses can be profitable. Success in a small Property Management business is not an accident. It requires both skills in a service or product area and acquisition of management and attitudinal competencies.

The purpose of this publication is to help you take stock of your interests, aptitudes and skills. Many people have good business ideas but not everyone has what it takes to succeed. If you are convinced that a profitable Property Management business is attainable, this publication will provide step-by-step guidance in development of the basic written business plan.

Information Gathering

A helpful tool for use in determining if you are ready to take the risks of an Property Management business operation is the SMA publication entitled *Going Into Business* (MP-12).

It will help you focus on the basic steps in information gathering and business planning.

Careful planning is required to research legal and tax issues, proper space utilization and to establish time management discipline. Inadequate or careless attention to development of a detailed business plan can be costly for you and your family in terms of lost time, wasted talent and disappearing dollars.

The Entrepreneurial Personality

A variety of experts have documented research that indicates that successful small business entrepreneurs have some common characteristics. How do you measure up? On this checklist, write a "Y" if you believe the statement describes you; a "N" if it doesn't; and a "U" if you can't decide:

_____ I have a strong desire to be my own boss.

_____ Win lose or draw, I want to be master of my own financial destiny.

_____ I have significant specialized business ability based on both my education and my experience.

_____ I have an ability to conceptualize the whole of a business; not just its individual parts, but how they relate to each other.

_____ I develop an inherent sense of what is "right" for a business and have the courage to pursue it.

_____ One or both of my parents were entrepreneurs; calculate risk-taking runs in the family.

_____ My life is characterized by a willingness and capacity to preserver.

_____ I possess a high level of energy, sustainable over long hours to make the business successful.

While not every successful Property Management business owner starts with a "Y" answer to all of these questions, three or four "N"s and "U"s should be sufficient reason for you to stop and give a second thought to going it alone. Many proprietors who sense entrepreneurial deficiencies seek extra training a support their limitations with help from a skilled team of business advisors such as accountants, bankers and attorneys.

Selecting a Business

A logical first step for the undecided is to list potential areas of personal background, special training, education and job experience, and special interests that could be developed into a business. Review the following list of activities which have proven marketable for others. On a scale of "0" (no interest or strength) to "10" (maximum interest or strength) indicate the potential for you and a total score for each activity.

Time Management

For both the novice and the experienced business person planning a small Property Management enterprise, an early concern requiring self-evaluation is time management.

It is very difficult for some people to make and keep work schedules even in a disciplined office setting. As your own boss the problem can be much greater. To determine how much time you can devote to your business, begin by drafting a weekly task timetable listing all current and potential responsibilities and the blocks of time required for each. When and how can business responsibilities be added without undue physical or mental stress on you or your family? Potential conflicts must be faced and resolved at the outset and as they occur, otherwise your business can become a nightmare. During the first year of operation, continue to chart, post and checkoff tasks on a daily, weekly and monthly basis.

Distractions and excuses for procrastination abound. It is important to keep both a planning and operating log. These tools will help avoid oversights and provide vital information when memory fails.

To improve the quality of work time, consider installation of a telephone line for the business and attaching an answering machine to take messages when you do not wish to be distracted or are away from your business. A business line has the added advantage of allowing you to have a business listing in the phone book and if you wish to buy it, an ad in the classified directory.

Is an Property Management Business Site Allowable?

Now you will want to investigate potential legal and community problems associated with operating the business. You should gather, read and digest specialized information concerning federal, state, county and municipal laws and regulations concerning Property Management business operations.

Check first! Get the facts in writing. Keep a topical file for future reference. Some facts and forms will be needed for your business plan. There may be limitations enforced that can make your planned business impossible or require expensive modifications to your property.

Items to be investigated, recorded and studied are:

TO DO   DONE

_____   _____   county or city zoning code restrictions
_____   _____   necessary permits and licenses for operation
_____   _____   state and local laws and codes regarding zoning
_____   _____   deed or lease restrictions such as covenants and
                          restrictive conditions of purchase

_____	_____	parking and customer access; deliveries
_____	_____	sanitation, traffic and noise codes
_____	_____	signs and advertising
_____	_____	state and federal code requirements for space, ventilation, heat and light
_____	_____	limitations on the number and type of workers. If not, check with the local Chamber of Commerce office
_____	_____	reservations that neighbors may have about a business next to or near them

Here are some ways to collect your information. Call or visit the zoning office at county headquarters or city hall. In some localities the city or county Office of Economic Development has print materials available to pinpoint key "code" items affecting a business.

Even in rural areas, the era of unlimited free enterprise is over. Although the decision makers may be in the state capital or in a distant regional office of a federal agency, check before investing in inventory, equipment or marketing programs. If in doubt, call the state office of Industrial Development or the nearest SBA district office. In some states the county agent or home demonstration agent will have helpful information concerning rural or farm business development.

Is the Business Site Insurable?

In addition to community investigations, contact your insurance company or agent. It is almost certain that significant changes will be required in your coverage and limits when you start a business. When you have written a good description of your business, call your agent for help in insuring you properly against new hazards resulting from your business operations such as:

- Fire, theft and casualty damage to inventories and equipment
- business interruption coverage
- fidelity bonds for employees
- liability for customers, vendors and others visiting the business
- workmen's compensation
- group health and life insurance
- product liability coverage if you make or sell a product; workmanship liability for services
- business use of vehicle coverage

Overall Property Management Site Evaluation

After you have gathered as much information as seems practical you may wish to evaluate several different locations. Here's a handy checklist. Using the "0" to "10" scale, grade these vital factors:

Factors to Consider

Factor	Grades 0-10
1. Customer convenience	_____
2. Availability of merchandise or raw materials	_____
3. Nearby competition	_____
4. Transportation availability and rates	_____
5. Quality and quantity of employees available	_____
6. Availability of parking facilities	_____

7. Adequacy of utilities (sewer, water, power, gas) _____

8. Traffic flow _____

9. Tax burden _____

10. Quality of police and fire services _____

11. Environmental factors _____

12. Physical suitability for future expansion _____

13. Provision for future expansion _____

14. Vendor delivery access _____

15. Personal convenience _____

16. Cost of operation _____

17. Other factors including how big you get without moving _____

TOTALS _____

Writing the Business Plan

Now that your research and plan development is nearing completion, it is time to move into action. If you are still in favor of going ahead, it is time to take several specific steps. The key one is to organize your dream scheme into a business plan.

What is it?

- As a business plan it is written by the Property Management business owner with outside help as needed
- It is accurate and concise as a result of careful study
- It explains how the business will function in the marketplace
- It clearly depicts its operational characteristics
- It details how it will be financed
- It outlines how it will be managed
- It is the management and financial "blueprint" for start-up and profitable operation
- It serves as a prospectus for potential investors and lenders

Why create it?

- The process of putting the business plan together, including the thought that you put in before writing it, forces you to take an objective, critical, unemotional look at your entire business proposal
- The finished written plan is an operational tool which, when properly used, will help you manage your business and work toward its success
- The completed business plan is a means for communicating your ideas to others and provides the basis for financing your business

Who should write it?

- The Property Management owner to the extend possible
- Seek assistance in weak areas, such as:
    — accounting
    — insurance
    — capital requirements
    — operational forecasting
    — tax and legal requirements

When should a business plan be used?

- To make crucial start-up decisions
- To reassure lenders or backers
- To measure operations progress
- To test planning assumptions
- As a basis for adjusting forecasts
- To anticipate ongoing capital and cash requirements
- As the benchmark for good operations management

Proposed Outline for Property Management Business Plan

This outline is suggested for a small proprietorship or family business. Shape it to fit *your* unique needs. For more complex manufacturing or franchise operations see the Resource section for other options.

Part I - Business Organization

Cover page:

A. Business name:
    Street address:
    Mailing address:
    Telephone number:
    Owner(s) name(s):

Inside pages:

B. Business form:
    (proprietorship, partnership, corporation)

    If incorporated (state incorporation)

    Include copies of key subsidiary documents in an appendix.

Remember even partnerships require written agreements of terms and conditions to avoid later conflicts and to establish legal entities and equities. Corporations require charters, articles of incorporation and bylaws.

Part II - Business Purpose and Function

In this section, write an accurate yet, concise description of the business. Describe the business you plan to start in narrative form.

What is the principal activity? Be specific. Give product or service description(s):

- retail sales?

- manufacturing?

- service?

- other?

How will it be started?

- a new start up

- the expansion of an existing business

- purchase of a going business

- a franchise operation

- actual or projected start up date

Why will it succeed? Promote your idea!

- how and why this business will be successful

- what is unique about your business

- what is its market "niche"

What is your experience in this business? If you have a current resume of your career, include it in an appendix and reference it here. Otherwise write a narrative here and include a resume in the finished product. If you lack specific experience, detail how you plan to gain it, such as training, apprenticeship or working with partners who have experience.

The Marketing Plan

The marketing plan is the core of your business rationale. To develop a consistent sales growth an Property Management business person much become knowledgeable about the market. To demonstrate your understanding, this section of the Property Management business plan should seek to concisely answer several basic questions:

Who is your market?

- Describe the profile of your typical customer
  Age?
  Male, female, both?
  How many in family?
  Annual family income?
  Location?
  Buying patterns?
  Reason to buy from you?

Other?

- Biographically describe your trading area (i.e., county, state, national)

- Economically describe your trading area: (single family, average earnings, number of children)

How large is the market?

- Total units or dollars?

- Growing _____ Steadily _____ Decreasing _____

- If growing, annual growth rate. _____

Who is your competition?

No small business operates in a vacuum. Get to know and respect the competition. Target your marketing plans. Identify direct competitors (both in terms of geography and product lines), and those who are similar or marginally comparative. Begin by listing names, addresses and products or service. Detail briefly but concisely the following information concerning each of your competitors:

- Who are the nearest ones?

- How are their businesses similar or competitive to yours?

- Do you have a unique "niche"? Describe it.

- How will your service or product be better or more saleable than your competitors?

- Are their businesses growing? Stable? Declining? Why?

- What can be learned from observing their operations or talking to their present or former clients?

- Will you have competitive advantages or disadvantages? Be honest!

What percent of the market will you penetrate?

1. estimate the market in total units or dollars

2. estimate your planned volume

3. amount your volume will add to total market

4. subtract 3 from 2

Item 4 represents the amount of your planned volume that must be taken away from the competition.

What pricing and sales terms are you planning?

The primary consideration in pricing a product or service is the value that it represents to the customer. If, on the previous checklist of features, your product is truly ahead of the field, you can command a premium price. On the other hand, if it is a "me too" product, you may have to "buy" a share of the market to get your foothold and then try to move price up later. This is always risky and difficult. One rule will always hold: ultimately, the market will set the price. If your selling price does not exceed your costs and expenses by the margin necessary to keep your business healthy, you will fail. Know your competitors pricing policies. Send a friend to comparison shop. Is there discounting? Special sales? Price leaders? Make some "blind" phone calls. Detail your pricing policy.

What is your sales plan?

Describe how you will sell, distribute or service what you sell. Be specific. Below are outlined some common practices:

Direct Sales - by telephone or in person. The tremendous growth of individual sales representatives who sell by party bookings, door to door, and through distribution of call back promotional campaigns suggests that careful research is required to be profitable.

Mail Order - Specialized markets for leisure time or unique products have grown as more two income families find less time to shop. Be aware of recent mail order legislation and regulation.

Franchising -

a. You may decide to either buy into someone else's franchise as a franchisee, or

b. Create your own franchise operation that sells rights to specific territories or product lines to others. Each will require further legal, financial and marketing research.

Management Plan
Who will do what?

Be sure to include four basic sets of information:

1. State a personal history of principals and related work, hobby or volunteer experience (include formal resumes in Appendix)

2. List and describe specific duties and responsibilities of each

3. List benefits and other forms of compensation for each

4. Identify other professional resources available to the business: Example: Accountant, lawyer, insurance broker, banker. Describe relationship of each to business: Example "Accountant available on part-time hourly basis, as needed, initial agreement calls for services not to exceed x hours per month at $xx.xx per hour."

To make this section graphically clear, start with a simple organizational chart that lists specific tasks and shows, *who* (type of person is more important than an individual name other than for principals) will do *what* indicate by arrows, work flow and lines of responsibility and/or communications. Consider the following examples:

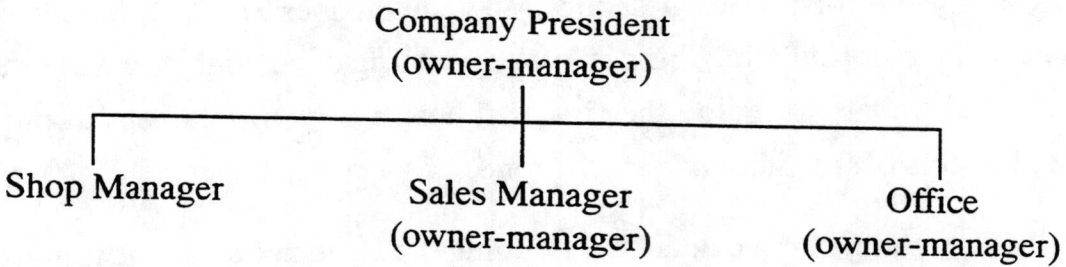

or like this?

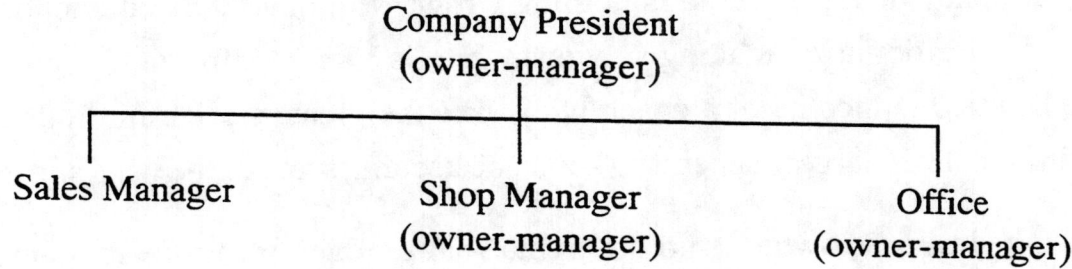

As the service business grows, its organization chart could look like this:

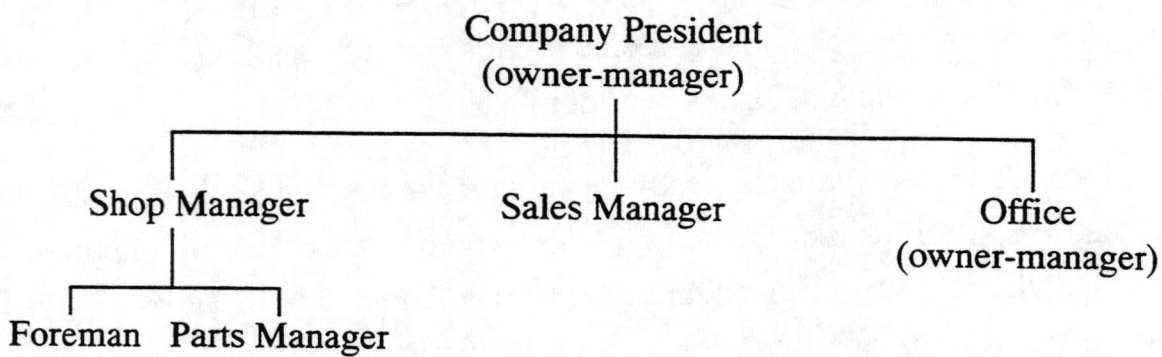

The Financial Plan

Clearly the most critical section of your business plan document is the financial plan. In formulating this part of the planning document, you will establish vital schedules that will guide the financial health of your business through the troubled waters of the first year and beyond.

Before going into the details of building the financial plan, it is important to realize that some basic knowledge of accounting is essential to the productive management of your business. If you are like most business owners, you probably have a deep and abiding interest in the product or services that you sell or intend to sell. You like to do what you do, and it is even more fulfilling that you are making money doing it. There is nothing wrong with that. Your conviction that what you are doing or making is worthwhile is vitally important to success. Nonetheless, the income of a coach who takes the greatest pride in producing a winning team will largely depend on someone keeping score of the wins and losses.

The business owner is no different. Your product or service may improve the condition of mankind for generations to come, but, unless you have access to an unlimited bankroll, you will fail if you don't make a profit. If you don't know what's going on in your business, you are not in a very good position to assure its profitability.

Most Property Management businesses will use the "cash" method of accounting with a system of record keeping that may be little more than a carefully annotated checkbook in which is recorded all receipts and all expenditures, backed up by a few forms of original entry (invoices, receipts, cash tickets). For a Sole Partnership, the business form assumed by this Management Aid, the very minimum of recorded information is that required to accurately complete the Federal Internal Revenue Service Form 1040, Schedule C. Other business types (partnerships, joint ventures, corporations) have similar requirements but use different tax forms.

If your business is, or will be, larger than just a small supplement to family income, you will need something more sophisticated. Stationery stores can provide you with several packaged small business account systems complete with simple journals and ledgers and detailed instructions in understandable language.

Should you feel that your accounting knowledge is so rudimentary that you will need professional assistance to establish your accounting system, the classified section of your telephone directory can lead you to a number of small business services that offer a complete range of accounting services. You can buy as much as you need, from a simple "pegboard" system all the way to computerized accounting, tax return service and monthly profitability consultation. Rates are reasonable for the services rendered and an investigative consultation will usually be free. Look under the heading, "Business Consultants," and make some calls.

Let's start by looking at the makeup of the financial plan for the business.

The Financial plan includes the following:

1. Financial Planning Assumptions - these are short statements of the conditions under which you plan to operate.

- Market health
- Date of start-up
- Sales build-up ($)
- Gross profit margin
- Equipment, furniture and fixtures required
- Payroll and other key expenses that will impact the financial plan

2. Operations Plan - Profit and Loss Projection - this is prepared for the first year's Budget. Appendix A-11.

3. Source of Funds Schedule - this shows the source(s) of your funds to capitalize the business and how they will be distributed among your fixed assets and working capital.

4. Pro Forma Balance Sheet - "Pro forma" refers to the fact that the balance sheet is before the fact, not actual. This form displays Assets, Liabilities and Equity of the business. This will indicate how much Investment will be required by the business and how much of it will be used as Working Capital in its operation.

5. Cash Flow Projection - this will forecast the flow of cash into and out of your business through the year. It helps you plan for staged purchasing, high volume months and slow periods.

Creating the Profit and Loss Projection.

Appendix A-11. Create a wide sheet of analysis paper with a three inch wide column at the extreme left and thirteen narrow columns across the page. Write at the top of the first page the planned name of your business. On the second line of the heading, write "Profit and Loss Projection." On the third line, write "First Year."

Then, note the headings on Appendix A-11 and copy them onto your 12-column sheet, copy the headings from the similar area on Exhibit A. Then follow the example set by Appendix A-11 and list all of the other components of your income, cost and expense structure. You may add or delete specific loans of expense to suit your business plan. Guard against consolidating too many types of expenses under one account lest you lose control of the components. At the same time, don't try to break down expenses so discretely that accounting becomes a nuisance instead of a management tool. Once again, Exhibit A provides ample detail for most businesses.

Now, in the small column just to the left of the first monthly column, you will want to note which of the items in the left-hand column are to be estimated on a monthly (M) or yearly (Y) basis. Items such as Sales, Cost of Sales and Variable expenses will be estimated monthly based on planned volume and seasonal or other estimated fluctuations. Fixed Expenses can usually be estimated on a yearly basis and divided by twelve to arrive at even monthly values. The "M" and "Y" designations will be used later to distinguish between variable and fixed expense.

Depreciation allowances for Fixed Assets such as production equipment, office furniture and machines, vehicles, etc. will be calculated from the Source of Funds Schedule.

Appendix A-11 describes line by line how the values on the Profit and Loss Projection are developed. Use this as your guide.

Source of Funds Schedule

To create this schedule, you will need to create a list of all the Assets that you intend to use in your business, how much investment each will require and the source of funds to capitalize them. A sample of such a list is shown below:

Asset	Cost	Source of Funds
Cash	$2,500	Personal savings
Accounts Receivable	3,000	From profits
Inventory	2,000	Vendor credit
Pickup truck	5,000	Currently owned
Packaging machine	10,000	Installment purchase
Office desk and chair	300	Currently owned
Calculator	75	Personal cash
Electric typewriter*	500	Personal savings

* A note about office equipment, test use or rent two or more brands that appear to meet your needs and select the one with which you feel most comfortable. Don't be afraid to ask others who have had to make this decision for advice. Compatibility of your system with those of potential typesetting services or printers should be of high considerations. If you are not quite sure, consider renting or leasing the equipment until you are. Service contracts on such complex electronic gear are usually a good insurance policy.

Before you leave your Source of Funds Schedule, indicate the number of months (years x 12) of useful life for depreciable fixed assets. (An example, the pickup truck, the packaging machine and the furniture and office equipment would be depreciable.) Generally, any individual item of equipment, furniture, fixtures, vehicles, etc., costing over $100 should be depreciated. For more information on allowances for depreciation, you can get free publications and assistance from your local Internal Revenue Service office. Divided the cost of each fixed asset item by the number or months over which it will be depreciated. You will need this data to enter as monthly depreciation on your Profit and Loss Projection. All of the data on the Source of Funds Schedule will be needed to create the Balance Sheet.

Creating the Pro Forma Balance Sheet

Appendix A-13. This is the Balance Sheet Form. There are a number of variations of this form and you may find it prudent to ask your banker for the form that the bank uses for small business. It will make it easier for them to evaluate the health of your business. Use this to get started and transfer the data to your preferred form later. Accompanying Appendix A-12 which describes line by line how to develop the Balance Sheet.

Even though you may plan to stage the purchase of some assets through the year, for the purpose of this pro forma Balance Sheet, assume that all assets will be provided at the start-up.

Cash Flow Projection

An important subsidiary schedule to your financial plan is a monthly Cash Flow Projection. Prudent business management practice is to keep no more cash in the business than is needed to operate it and to protect it from catastrophe. In most small businesses, the problem is rarely one of having too much cash. A Cash Flow Projection is made to advise management of the amount of cash that is going to be absorbed by the operation of the business and compares it against the amount that will be available.

SBA has created an excellent form for this purpose and it is shown as Appendix B. Your projection should be prepared on 13-column analysis paper to allow for a twelve-month projection. Appendix B represents a line by line description and explanation of the components of the Cash Flow Projection which provides a step-by-step method of preparation.

Resources

U.S. Small Business Administration
Office of Business Development

Business Development Publication
MP15

Notes

Notes _____

Chapter 7

Managing The Business

Delegating work, responsibility, and authority is difficult in a small business because it means letting others make decisions which involved spending the owner/manager's money. At a minimum, he should delegate enough authority to get the work done, to allow assistants to take initiative, and to keep the operation moving in his absence. Coaching those who carry responsibility and authority in self-improvement is essential and emphasis in allowing competent assistants to perform in their own style rather than insisting that things be done exactly as the owner/manager would personally do them is important. "Let others take care of the details" is the meaning of delegating work and responsibility. In theory, the same principles for getting work done through other people apply whether you have 25 employees and one top assistant or 150 to 200 employees and several keymen yet, putting the principles into practice is often difficult.

Delegation is perhaps the hardest job owner/managers have to learn. Some never do. They insist on handling many details and work themselves into early graves. Others pay lip service to the idea but actually run a one-man shop. They give their assistants many responsibilities but little or no authority. Authority is the fuel that makes the machine go when you delegate word and responsibility. If an owner/manager is to run a successful company, he must delegate authority properly. How much authority is proper depends on your situation. At a minimum, you should delegate enough authority: (1) to get the work done, (2) to allow keymen to take initiative, (3) to keep things going in your absence.

The person who fills a key management spot in the organization must either be a manager or be capable of becoming one. A manager's chief job is to plan, direct, and coordinate the work of others. He should possess the three "I's" — Initiative, Interest, and Imagination. The manager of a department must have enough self-drive to start and keep things moving. Personality traits must be considered. A keyman should be strong-willed enough to overcome opposition when necessary.

When you manage through others, it is essential that you keep control. You do it by holding a subordinate responsible for his actions and checking the results of those actions. In controlling your assistants, try to strike a balance. You should not get into a keyman's operations so closely that you are "in his hair" nor should you be so far removed that you lose control of things.

You need feedback to keep yourself informed. Reports provide a way to get the right kind of feedback at the right time. This can be daily, weekly, or monthly depending on how soon you need the information. Each department head can report his progress, or lack of it, in the unit of production that is appropriate for his activity; for example, items packed in the shipping room, sales per territory, hours of work per employee.

For the owner/manager, delegation does not end with good control. It involves coaching as well, because management ability is not required automatically. You have to teach it. Just as important, you have to keep your managers informed just as you would be if you were doing their jobs.

Part of your job is to see that they get the facts they need for making their decisions. You should be certain that you convey your thinking when you coach your assistants. Sometimes words can be inconsistent with thoughts. Ask questions to make sure that the listener understands your meaning. In other words, delegation can only be effective when you have good communications.

Sometimes an owner/manager finds himself involved in many operational details even though he does everything that is necessary for delegation of responsibility. In spite of defining authority, delegation, keeping control, and coaching, he is still burdened with detailed work. Usually, he had failed to do one vital thing. He has refused to stand back and let the wheels turn.

If the owner/manager is to make delegation work, he must allow his subordinates freedom to do things their way. He and the company are in trouble if he tries to measure his assistants by whether they do a particular task exactly as he would do it. They should be judged by their results — not their methods. No two persons react exactly the same in every situation. Be prepared to see some action taken differently from the way in which you would do it even though your policies are well defined. Of course, if an assistant strays too far from policy, you need to bring him back in line. You cannot afford second-guessing.

You should also keep in mind that when an owner/manager second-guesses his assistants, he risks destroying their self-confidence. If the assistant does not run his department to your satisfaction and if his shortcomings cannot be overcome, then replace him. But when results prove his effectiveness, it is good practice to avoid picking at each move he makes.

Notes

Chapter 8

Business Resource Information

Books
Finding Your Niche, by Lawrence J. Pino. 1994, Berkley Publishing Group, New York

Finding Your Perfect Work: The New Career Guide to Making a Living, Creating a Life,
  by Paul and Sarah Edwards. 1996 J.P. Tarcher, Los Angeles, CA.

*The Pathfinder: How to Choose or Change Your Career for a Lifetime of Satisfaction and
Success,* by Nicholas Lore. 1997, Fireside, New York.

Which Business? Help in Selecting Your New Venture,
  by Nancy Drescher. 1997, Oasis Press, Grants Pass, OR.

Books for Start-Up Business
Anatomy of a Business Plan, 3rd ed.,
  by Linda Pinson and Jerry Jinnett. 1996, Upstart Publishing Company, Dover, NH.

How to Write a Successful Business Plan,
  by Jerre Lewis and Leslie Renn. 1997, Lewis & Renn Assocs., 10315 Harmony Dr.,
  Interlochen, MI 49643. $14.95 + $3 postage and handling.

Growing Your Home-Based Business,
  by Kim T. Gordon. 1992, Prentice Hall, Upper Saddle River, NJ.

Surefire Strategies for Growing Your Home-Based Business,
  by David Schaefer. 1997, Dearborn Trade, Chicago, IL.

Your First Business: How to Really Start Your Own Business This Year, by Mainstay Company.
  1997, 511 Avenue of the Americas, Suite 350, New York, NY 10011-8436. Send $19.95
  (includes postage and handling) by check or money order.

Books for Financing Businesses
   Launching Your Home-Based Business: How to Successfully Plan, Finance, and Grow Your New Venture, by David H. Bangs, Jr. 1997, Dearborn Trade, Chicago, IL.

   Minding Her Own Business: The Self-Employed Woman's Guide to Taxes and Record keeping, by Jan Zobel. 1998, Easthill Press, Oakland, CA.

   Small Business Financial Resource Guide (booklet). Write to: The National Federation of Independent Business (NFIB), 600 Maryland Ave., SW, #700, Washington, DC 20024. <http://www.nfibonline.com>

Books for Internet Sites
   Cheapskate's Guide to Building a Web Site with Windows 95/NT, by Pete Palmer. 1998, Prentice Hall Professional, Upper Saddle River, NJ.

Books on Legal Structure for Businesses
   Choosing a Legal Structure for Your Business, by Stuart A. Handmaker. 1997, Prentice Hall Trade, Upper Saddle River, NJ.

Business Plan Guide
   Entrepreneur's Business Guide, Writing an Effective Business Plan. (800) 421-2300. $69 + shipping and handling.

Business Plan Software
   Palo Alto Software, 144 East 14th Avenue, Eugene, OR 97401 (888) 752-6776 <http://www.palo-alto.com/>

   Microsoft Corporation, Redmond, WA 98052 (800) 426-9400; <http://www.microsoft.com>

   Arden, Lynie, The Work at Home Source Book. Boulder, CO: Live Oak Publications, 1996.

   Bautista, Veltisezar. How to Build a Successful One-Person Business. Farmington Hills, MI: Bookhaus Publishers, 1995.

Liraz Publishing. The Entrepreneur Test. The Managing a Small Business CD-ROM:
Liraz Publishing Co., 1996.

Liraz, Publishing. The 30 Best Inspiring Anecdotes of All Times. The Managing a Small
Business CD-ROM: Liraz Publishing Co., 1996.

Lord, David. National Business Employment Weekly Guide to Self-Employment.
New York: John Wiley and Sons, 1996.

Ramsey, Dan. 101 Best Weekend Businesses. Franklin Lakes, NJ: Career Press, 1996.

Government Resources - Federal
Bureau of the Census, Customer Services
Data User Services Division
Suitland and Silver Hill roads, Washington, DC 20233
(301) 763-8576; <http://www.census.gov>
Provides statistics

Bureau of Labor Statistics
(202) 606-6378
<http://www.bls.gov>
Also provides statistics

Consumer Information Center
P.O. Box 100 Pueblo, CO 81002
<http://www.peublo.gsa.gov>
Send for free Consumer Information Catalog. You can order free or low cost information on
many topics, including small business information.

Internal Revenue Service
4300 Caroline Ave., Richmond, VA 23222
(800) 829-1040
<http://.www.securetax.com>, <http://www.irs.ustreas.gov> (other state and federal tax forms)

Office of Women's Business Ownership
Small Business Administration
409 Third St. SW, 6th Floor, Washington, DC 20416
(202) 205-6673; <http://www/sba/gov/womenbusiness
Send for a free packet of business information of interest to women.

Service Corps of Retired Executives Association (SCORE)
409 Third St., SW, 4th Floor, Washington, DC 20024
<http://www.sba.gov/SCORE/program.html>
A nonprofit association funded by the SBA, made up of mostly retired men and women who worked in business management. Services are free and they provide small business counseling. Write for SCORE contacts in your area or call your local SBDC.

U.S. Patent and Trademark Office
Washington, DC 20231
(703) 308-HELP [4357]; <http://uspto.gov>

U.S. Small Business Administration (SBA)
409 Third St., SW, Washington, DC 20416
This is the primary source for government assistance for small businesses. Their regional and Small Business Development Centers offer free or low-cost assistance, seminars, and workshops. They also offer many helpful publications.

Helpful Resource Book/Directories
    These can usually be found in college or larger public libraries.

2001 Sources for Financing a Small Business
    Book of Business Plans; National Directory of Women-Owned Firms;
    Small Business Sourcebook, Gale Research.

Directory of Directories, Gale Research, Detroit, MI.
    Dun's Business Rankings

Internet Business 500: The Top Essential Sites for Business, by Ryan Bernard.
    1995, Ventana Communications Group, Inc., Research Triangle Park, NC.

Thomas's Lists of Manufacturers, <http://www/thomasregister.com>

U.S. Industrial Outlook
    See also *A Directory of National Women's Organizations* published by:
    The National Council for Research on Women
    The Sara Delano Roosevelt Memorial House
    47-49 E. 65th St.
    New York, NY 10021

A Concise Guide To Starting Your Own Business

Guide Overview

A concise overview of the complete guide to starting and operating a successful business.

The following topics are presented:

- Business Plan for Small Businesses.
- Getting Started
- Deciding Where To Start The Business
- Business Patronage Statistics
- Site Location
- Site Selection Criteria — Some General Questions.
- Choosing The Proper Method of Organization
- What Is A Corporation?
- Estimating Start-up Costs
- Preparing An Income Statement
- Preparing A Balance Sheet
- Marketing The Business
- Marketing Planning — An Outline for Marketing
- Advertising Media
- Management and Getting The Work Done
- Sample Organization Chart
- Summary of the Business Plan
- Guide Summary
- Reference Materials

Business Plan for Small Businesses

I. Type of Business

II. Location

III. Target Market

IV. Planning Process

V. Organizational Structure

VI. Staffing Procedures

VII. Control

VIII. Market Strategy

IX. Financial Planning

X. Budgeted Balance Sheet

XI. Budgeted Income Statement

XII. Budgeted Cash Flow Statement

XIII. Break-even Chart

Page A-4

Getting Started

Following is a list of what you need to accomplish to insure that your business endeavor will head in the right direction.

1. Define your educational background and work experience

2. Survey all basic types of businesses.

3. Define what type of business matches your experience and educational background.

4. Choose only the business that you would like to own and operate.

5. Define what products or services your business will be marketing.

6. Define who will be using your products/services.

7. Define why they will be purchasing your products/services.

8. List all competitors in your marketing area.

Deciding Where to Start the Business

Will your business fulfill a need in the area you plan to bring your business to? This section provides you with some important information you need to examine before taking your ideas any further:

1. Decide where you want to live.

2. Choose several areas that would match your priorities.

3. Use the list that follows as a guide to see if your location will match the estimated population needed to support your business. The numbers which follow the type of business indicate the typical number of inhabitants per year.

Business Patronage Statistics

Food Stores
Grocery Stores 1,534
Meat and Fish
  (Sea Food) Markets . . . 17,876
Candy, Nut, and
  Confectionery Stores . . 31,409
Retail Bakeries 12,563
Dairy Products Stores . . . 41,587

Eating and Drinking
Restaurant, Lunch Rooms . 1,583
Cafeterias 19,341
Refreshment Places 3,622
Drinking Places 2,414

General Merchandise
Variety Stores 10,373
General Merchandise 9,837

Apparel/Accessories Stores
Women's Ready-To-
  Wear Stores 7,102
Women's Accessory and
  Specialty Stores 25,824
Men's and Boy's Clothing
  and Furnishings 11,832
Family Clothing 16,890
Shoe Stores 9,350

Furniture, Home Furnishings, and Equipment Stores
Furniture Stores 7,210
Floor Covering 29,543
Drapery, Curtains, and
  Upholstery Stores 62,585
House, Appliances 12,485
Radios and TV's 20,346
Record Shops 112,144
Musical Instruments 46,332

Building Materials, Hardware, and Farm Equipment Dealers
Lumber and other Building
  Materials Dealers 8,124
Paint, Glass, and Wallpaper
  Stores 22,454
Hardware Stores 10,206
Farm Equipment Dealers . 14,793

Automotive Dealers
Motor Vehicle Dealers,
  New and Used Cars 6,000
Motor Vehicle Dealers,
  Used Cars only 17,160
Tire, battery, and
  Accessory Dealers 8,800

Boat Dealers 61,500

Household Trailer Dealers . 44,746

Gasoline Service Stations . . . 1,395

Miscellaneous
Antique and Secondhand
  Stores 17,170
Book and Stationery Stores 28,580
Drugstores 4,268
Florists 13,531
Fuel Oil Dealers 25,000
Garden Supply Stores . . . 65,000
Gift, Novelty Shops 26,000
Hobby, Toy, and Game
  Shops 61,000
Jewelry Stores 13,400
Optical Goods Stores 62,800
Sporting Goods Store 27,000

From *Starting and Managing a Small Business of Your Own, 1973;*
Small Business Administration, Washington, DC

Page A-6

Site Location

1. Define your number of inhabitants per store.

2. Locate several sites/locations that will match your inhabitants per stores.

3. Define population and its growth potential.

4. Define local ordinances and zoning regulations that you will need in order to start your type of business.

5. Define your trading area and all competitors in your trading area.

6. Define parking need, for your kind of business.

7. Define special needs, etc., lighting, heating, ventilation.

8. Define rental cost of site/location.

9. Define why customers will come to your site/location.

10. Define the future of your site/location as to population growth.

11. Define your space needs and match with site/location selection.

12. Define the image of your business and make sure it matches your site/location.

Site Selection Criteria — Some General Questions

- Is the site centrally located to reach my market?

- What is the transportation availability and what are the rates?

- What provisions for future expansion can I make:

- What is the topography of the site (slope and foundation)?

- What is the housing availability for workers and managers?

- What environmental factors (schools, cultural, community atmosphere) might affect my business and my employees?

- What will the quality of this site be in 5 years, 10 years, 25 years?

- What is my estimate of this site in relation to my major competitor?

- What other media are available for advertising? How many radio and television stations are there?

- Is the Quantity and quality of available labor concentrated in a given area in the city or town? If so, is commuting a way of living in that city or town?

- Is the city centrally located to my suppliers?

- What are the labor conditions, including such things as relationships with the business community and average wages and salaries paid?

- Is the local business climate healthy, or are business failures especially high in the area?

- What about tax requirements? Is there a city business tax? Income tax? What is the property tax rate? Is there a personal property tax? Are there other special taxes?

- Is the available police and fire protection adequate?

- Is the city or town basically well planned and managed in terms of such items as electric power, sewage, and paved streets and sidewalks?

Choosing the Proper Method of Organization

Listed below are legal forms of business available to the small business entrepreneur:

Sole Proprietorship

Advantages
- Simple to start
- All profits to owner
- Owner in direct control
- Easy entry and exit
- Taxed as individual

Disadvantages
- Unlimited liability
- "Jack-of-all-trades"
- Capital requirement limited
- Limited life
- Employee turn-over

Partnership

Advantages
- Easy to originate
- Credit rating
- Talent combination
- Legal Contract

Disadvantages
- Unlimited liability
- Misunderstandings
- Partner withdrawal
- Regulations

Corporation

Advantages
- Limited liability
- Expansion potential
- Transfer of ownership
- Retain employees

Disadvantages
- Double taxation
- Charter restrictions
- Employee motivation
- Legal regulations

What Is A Corporation?

A corporation is an artificial being, invisible, intangible, and existing only in contemplation of the law," wrote Chief Justice John Marshall. In other words, the corporation exists as a separate entity apart from its owners, the shareholders. It makes contracts; it is liable; it pays taxes. It is a "legal person".

The corporation is the most complex of the three major forms of business ownership. The corporation stands as a separate legal entity in the eyes of the law. The life of the corporation is independent of the owners' lives. Because the owners, called shareholders, are legally separate from the corporation, they can sell their interests in the business without affecting the continuation of the business. When a corporation is founded, it accepts the regulations and restrictions placed on it by the state in which it is incorporated and any other state in which it chooses to do business. Generally, the corporation must report its financial operations to the state's attorney general on an annual basis.

Page A-10

Estimating Start-up Costs

Item	Amount
Fixtures and Equipment	$ _____
Building & Land (If Needed)	_____
Store and/or Office Supplies	_____
Remodeling and Decorating	_____
Deposits on Utilities	_____
Insurance	_____
Installation of Fixtures	_____
Legal Fees	_____
Professional Fees	_____
Telephone	_____
Rental	_____
Salaries and Wages	_____
Inventory if Retailing	_____
Licenses and Permits	_____
Advertising and Promotion	_____
TOTAL Estimated Start-up Cost	$_____

Preparing An Income Statement

What is an Income Statement?

The income statement shows the income received and the expenses incurred over a period of time. Income received (sales) comes essentially from the sales of the merchandise or service which your business is formed to sell. Expenses incurred are the expired costs that have been incurred during the same period of time.

Plan A Budgeted Income Statement For One Year

1. Project Total Sales
2. Estimate Total Expenditures
3. Example Listed Below for Income Statement

Percents	1	2	3	4	5	6	7	8	9	10	11	12
Sales												
Cost of Sales												
Gross Profit												
Expenditure												
Rent Expense												
Supplies												
Wages/Salaries												
Utilities												
Insurance												
Depreciation												
Interest												
Miscellaneous												
Net Profit												

Preparing A Balance Sheet

What is a Balance Sheet?

The balance sheet shows the assets, liabilities and owner's net worth in a business as of a given date.

- Assets are the things owned by your business, including both physical things and claims against others.
- Liabilities are the amounts owned to others, the creditors of the firm.
- Net worth or owner's equity is the owner's claim to the assets after liabilities are accounted for.

A Budgeted Balance Sheet For One Year

- List all your business property at their cost to you: these are your assets.
- List all debts, or what your business owes on all your property; these are your liabilities.
- Take your total property balance (Assets), and subtract the total amount you owe (Liabilities).
- The balance is what you own in your business called (Owner's equity).
- Add Total Liabilities (2) & Total Owner's Equity (3).
- Listed on the next page is an example of a balance sheet.

NAME OF BUSINESS
BALANCE SHEET
DATE

ASSETS

Current Assets
  Cash _____
  Accounts Receivable _____
Merchandise Inventories _____
    TOTAL CURRENT ASSETS
        _____

Fixed Assets
  Land _____
  Building _____
  Equipment _____
    TOTAL FIXED ASSETS
        TOTAL ASSETS _____
            1). _____

LIABILITIES

Current Liabilities
  Accounts Payable _____
  Note Payable _____
  Payroll Taxes Payable _____
    TOTAL CURRENT LIABILITIES
        _____

Long-term Liabilities
  Mortgage Payable _____
  Long-term Note _____
    TOTAL LONG-TERM LIABILITIES
        TOTAL LIABILITIES _____
            2). _____

OWNER'S EQUITY
  Proprietor's Capital
            3). _____

        TOTAL LIABILITIES & OWNER'S EQUITY   (2 &3). _____

Marketing The Business

1. Define Your Market
   - Type of Customers
   - Age, Income, Occupation of your customers
   - Type of Trading Area

2. Promotion of Your Business
   - Advertising
   - Setting your Image

3. Customer Policy Plan
   - Develop a Customer Profile
   - Customer Services
   - Customer Needs

4. Pricing Your Products/Services
   - Know all your Costs
   - Know your Profit Margin
   - Know Competitor's Price
   - Know what Return you want on your Investment

5. Sales Promotion
   - Coupons
   - Contests
   - Displays
   - Demonstrations
   - Giveaways
   - Banners

6. Public Relations
   - Newspaper Article
   - Contact Trade Association
   - Radio Promotion
   - TV Promotion

7. Segmentation of your Market
   - Age
   - Occupation
   - Income
   - Location
   - Education
   - Hobbies

Marketing Planning

Outline for Marketing

I. Product/Service Concept:
   a. Name of product or service
   b. Descriptive characteristics of product or service
   c. Unit sales
   d. Analysis of market trends

II. Number of Customers in your Market Area:
   a. Profile of customers
   b. Average customer expenditure
   c. Total market

III. Your Market Potential:
   a. Total market divided by competition
   b. Total market multiplied by percent who will buy your product

IV. Needs of Customers:
   a. Identification
   b. Pleasure
   c. Social approval
   d. Personal interest
   e. Price

V. Direct Marketing Sources:
   a. Trade magazines
   b. Trade associations
   c. Small Business Administration (SBA)
   d. Government Publications
   e. Yellow pages
   f. Marketing directories

VI Customer Profile:
   a. Geographical
   b. Gender
   c. Age range
   d. Income brackets
   e. Occupation
   f. Educational level

Page A-16

Advertising Media

Medium	Market Coverage	Type of Audience
Daily newspaper	Single community or entire metro area: zoned editions sometimes available	General
Weekly newspaper	Single Community	Residents
Telephone Directory	Geographical area or occupational field served by the directory	Active shoppers for goods or services
Direct mail audience	Controlled by the advertiser	Controlled
Radio audience	Definable market area	Selected
Television audience	Definable market area surrounding TV Stations	Various
Outdoor	Entire metro area	General auto drivers
Magazine	Entire metro area or magazine region	Selected audience

Management and Getting the Work Done

1. Define your objective for starting your business.

2. Define your goals: profit growth for first three years.

3. Develop an organization chart of your business.

4. Define your personal needs.
   - Hiring proper employees
   - Training employees
   - Motivation

5. Define all responsibility for each person in your business.

6. Define all authority.
   - Who will hire and fire?
   - Who will select and train all personnel?
   - Who will keep the important records as to inventory, purchasing, sales records, cash records, etc.?

7. Define all laws and regulations that will be requirements for operating your business.

8. Review all duties and tasks with all your employees.

9. Write a summary of all the important tasks that you want to finish in your first year in business.

Sample Organization Chart

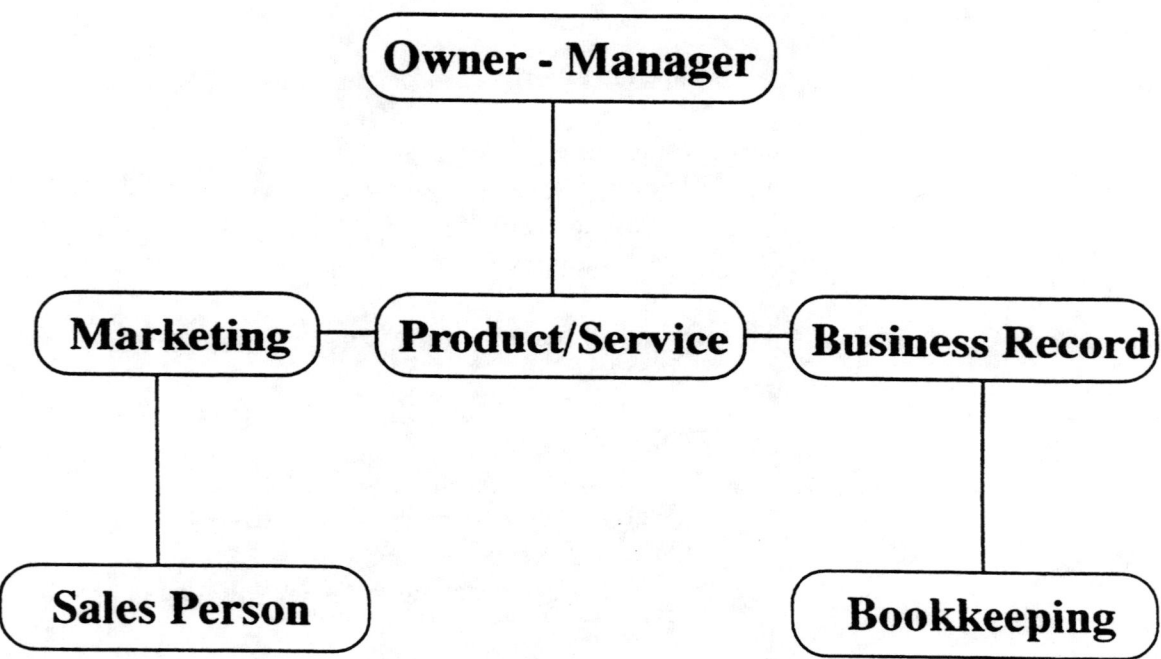

Summary of The Business Plan

Name of Business
BUSINESS PLAN
Date

1. Define your business
   - Name all principals
   - Address and phone number

2. Define your products or services

3. Define your market

4. Define your site or location

5. Advertising Plan
   - Budget
   - Media

6. Chart of Start-up cost

7. Worksheet of Income Statement
   - Revenue/Income
   - Expenses

8. Worksheet of Balance Sheet
   - Assets (Property)
   - Capital (Owner's Equity)
   - Liabilities (Debts)

9. Personnel Outline
   - Number of Employees
   - Staffing & Training

10. Management Organization
    - Organization Chart
    - Evaluation Policy
    - Job Profile

11. Special Statement
    - 3-Year Sales Schedule
    - Cash Flow
    - 3-Year Expense Schedule

Page A-20

Appendix A Summary

1. Contact your State Commerce Department for guidelines in starting your business.

2. Contact your City/County Clerk for guidelines in starting your business.

3. Contact all other Governmental Centers that will furnish you all the legal regulations and tax laws that will effect your business.
   - State Government
   - Internal Revenue Service
   - State Employment Security Commission
   - Department of Treasury
   - City Governmental Units

        a. Fire
        b. Police
        c. Zoning
        d. Building Permits
        e. Health
        f. Water & Sewage

4. Township Government
   - Local Legal Requirements
   - Local Taxes
   - Local Health Permits
   - Local Zoning Laws

**Reference
Materials**

Management Aids Titles

Contact the

**Small Business Administration
P.O. Box 15434
Fort Worth, TX 76119**

for the following booklets:

- Number 2.025   Thinking About Going Into Business
- Number 2.010   Planning and Goal Setting For Business
- Number 1.016   Sound Cash Management
- Number 1.001   The A.B.C's. of Borrowing
- Number 1.008   Break-even Analysis
- Number 2.022   Business Plan For Service Firms
- Number 2.023   Business Plans for Retail Firms

Notes _____

Appendix B

HOUSEHOLD NEEDS

Many small business start-ups fail due to their inability to support their owners. Rarely do new businesses support their owners from the start. However, many individuals fail to recognize this fact. In addition, then, to a sound business plan, it is necessary for an owner to project the household cash needs month-by-month for the first three years of the business' operation. As a new business owner, you should be able to support yourself until your new business is able to support you in a manner to which you are accustomed.

MONTHLY HOUSEHOLD CASH NEEDS

Regular NON-BUSINESS Income
Spouse's salary _____
Investment income _____
Social security _____
Other income _____
Retirement benefits _____
Less taxes _____
Net monthly income _____

Regular Monthly Expenses

Housing
　　Mortgage/Rent _____
　　Utilities _____
　　Homeowner's insurance _____
　　Property taxes _____
　　Home repairs _____

Living Expenses
　　Groceries _____
　　Telephone _____
　　Tuition _____
　　Transportation _____
　　Meals _____
　　Child care _____
　　Medical expenses _____
　　Clothing _____
　　Personal _____

Insurance Premiums
　　Life insurance _____
　　Disability insurance _____
　　Auto insurance _____
　　Medical insurance _____

Debt Repayment
　　Auto loans _____
　　Consumer debt _____

Discretionary Expenses
　　Entertainment _____
　　Vacation _____
　　Gifts _____
　　Retirement contributions _____
　　Investment savings _____
　　Charitable contributions _____
　　Dues, magazines, etc. _____
　　Professional fees _____
　　Other _____

Total Monthly Expenses _____

Monthly Surplus/Deficit _____

Total Year Surplus/Deficit _____
(Monthly x 12)

Available Assets to Cover Deficit
　　Checking accounts _____
　　Savings accounts _____
　　Money market accounts _____
　　Personal credit lines _____
　　Marketable securities _____
　　Lump-sum retirement/
　　　severance _____
　　Other assets _____

Total Assets _____

NEEDED RESERVES
　　Total Assets-Deficit _____

PERSONAL FINANCIAL STATEMENT

This is a picture of your personal financial condition to date. It is a very important part of any loan application and/or interview, especially when a loan for a projected new business is under consideration.

PERSONAL FINANCIAL STATEMENT

_____   _____ , 19 _____

Assets
Cash
Savings accounts _____
Stocks, bonds, other securities _____
Accounts/Notes receivable _____
Life insurance cash value _____
Rebates/Refunds _____
Autos/Other vehicles _____
Real estate _____
Vested pension plan/Retirement accounts _____
Other assets _____

TOTAL ASSETS $ _____

Liabilities

Accounts payable _____
Contracts payable _____
Notes payable _____
Taxes _____
Real estate loans _____
Other liabilities _____

TOTAL LIABILITIES $ _____

TOTAL ASSETS $ _____

LESS TOTAL LIABILITIES $ _____

NET WORTH $ _____

BALANCE SHEET

A balance sheet is a current financial statement. It is a dollars and cents description of your business (existing or projected) which lists all of its assets and liabilities.

BALANCE SHEET

_____ _____ , 19 _____

	YEAR 1	YEAR II
Current Assets		
Cash		
Accounts receivable		
Inventory		
Fixed Assets		
Real estate		
Fixtures and equipment		
Vehicles		
Other Assets		
License		
Goodwill		
TOTAL ASSETS	$_____	$_____
Current Liabilities		
Notes payable (due within 1 year)	$_____	$_____
Accounts payable		
Accrued expenses		
Taxes owed		
Long-Term Liabilities		
Notes payable (due after 1 year)		
Other		
TOTAL LIABILITIES	$_____	$_____
NETWORTH (ASSETS minus LIABILITIES)	$_____	$_____

TOTAL LIABILITIES plus NET WORTH should equal ASSETS

PROFIT AND LOSS STATEMENT

A profit and loss statement is a detailed earnings statement for the previous full year (if you are already in business). Existing businesses are also required to show a profit and loss statement for the current period to the date of the balance sheet.

PROJECTED PROFIT AND LOSS STATEMENT

	Month 1	Month 2	Month 3	Month 4	Month 5	Month 6	Month 7	Month 8	Month 9	Month 10	Month 11	Month 12
Total Net Sales												
Cost of Sales												
GROSS PROFIT												
Controllable Expenses												
Salaries												
Payroll taxes												
Security												
Advertising												
Automobile												
Dues and subscriptions												
Legal and accounting												
Office supplies												
Telephone												
Utilities												
Miscellaneous												
Total Controllable Expenses												
Fixed Expenses Depreciation												
Insurance												
Rent												
Taxes and licenses												
Loan payments												
Total Fixed Expenses												
TOTAL EXPENSES												
NET PROFIT (LOSS) **(before taxes)**												

CASH FLOW PROJECTIONS

A cash flow projection is a forcast of the cash (checks or money orders) a business anticipates receiving and disbursing during the course of a month. Well managed, the cash flow should be sufficient to meet the cash requirements for the following month.

CASH FLOW PROJECTIONS

	Start-up or prior to loan	Month 1	Month 2	Month 3	Month 4	Month 5	Month 6	Month 7	Month 8	Month 9	Month 10	Month 11	Month 12	TOTAL
Cash (beginning of month														
Cash on hand														
Cash in bank														
Cash in investments														
Total Cash														
Income (during month)														
Cash sales														
Credit sales payment														
Investment income														
Loans														
Other cash income														
Total Income														
TOTAL CASH AND INCOME														
Expenses (during month														
Inventory or new material														
Wages (including owner's)														
Taxes														
Equipment expense														
Overhead														
Selling expense														
Transportation														
Loan repayment														
Other cash expenses														
TOTAL EXPENSES														
CASH FLOW EXCESS (end of month)														
CASH FLOW CUMULATIVE (Monthly)														

Getting Down to Business...

How to Start & Manage a Property Management Business

**An Instructional Guide
for Creating a Small Business
by Jerre G. Lewis, M.A.
and Leslie D. Renn, M.S.**

Notes

Property Management

Today 52 million Americans rent the place that they call home — be it a single family dwelling, apartment, duplex, triplex, townhouse, or even a mobile home. The owners of these rental buildings range from giant corporations to cookie-baking grandmothers or young married couples with babies. Large or small, these owners have one common purpose; the desire to make a good return on their invested dollars.

Making money as a property owner depends both on making wise initial investment decisions *and* on having an ability to manage property. this holds true whether a person owns 25 apartment buildings, 50 living units, or one house. Today property values and rents have reached record levels, making many people eager to own income-producing property. But costs, too, have climbed, and professional management is needed to turn a profit. A poorly managed or maintained building could increase very little, or even decrease, in value, and the owner might even fall behind in mortgage payments and lose the structure altogether. According to one real estate professional, poor property management has caused more failure for owners of income real estate in the 1970's than any other single factor -- including rent controls, overbuilding, and other economic problems.

Ideally, the owner of a small property should have some of the skills of a carpenter, plumber, electrician, locksmith, roofer, gardener, custodian, purchasing agent, bill collector, financial analyst, real estate broker — and diplomat. Fortunately, numerous evening courses or weekend seminars on property management are available through apartment associations and at many colleges and universities.

Dealing with tenants and their foibles can create king-size headaches. And a harried owner groans, "I've had phone calls at *midnight* from tenants who expected me to race right down and change a light bulb for them. "

Despite such drawbacks, owning and managing a rental property can be a profitable sideline or career for a person who tackles the field in a professional manner. Coping with the day-to-day problems may not be quite the easy road to riches that it seems from the outside, but investing in income-producing property can be a lucrative venture for the responsible individual.

Improvements and Maintenance:

When an individual acquires income property, the first order of business usually is to tackle needed repairs and renovation. Almost every building needs *some* exterior and interior improvements and decorating to make it more attractive and easily rentable. Selection of the first jobs to undertake depends on the condition of the building. Obviously, a leaky roof, clogged plumbing, or sagging foundation will need work before anything else, and any violations of fire or safety codes must be corrected immediately.

In many areas, the building owner can perform any of these repairs personally. But building codes in some large areas like Los Angeles require that plumbing and electrical work be performed by a licensed contractor, although an owner may either personally do some carpentry work or hire unlicensed laborers for such alterations. For all major renovation work a local building permit will usually be necessary and an inspection required on completion. A telephone call to the relevant city or county building inspectors will clarify the need for such a permit and the procedure for obtaining one.

Before any contractor is hired, competitive bids should be obtained, in writing and with specified beginning and completion dates. "And remember, the lowest bid isn't always the best," cautions one owner. "Make sure you know exactly what you are getting for your money."

Exterior:

For the typical dwelling that needs only minor repairs or sprucing up, the building exterior is usually the best place to start. An attractive exterior projects a better image for present residents and helps attract new ones.

One of the best ways to obtain innovative ideas for improving the exterior of a building or complex is to study attractive buildings in the area, noting what is particularly pleasing to the eye and worthy of emulation.

Landscaping should be one of the first exterior chores since the sooner the planting is completed, the faster the garden will grow. Trees and hardy low-maintenance plants native to the region provide the best and fastest cover. Often owners can get good ideas by examining landscaping in the community or by consulting local nurseries or landscape gardeners.

Interior:

Nothing seems to improve the interior of an apartment so much as new paint or wallpaper and new floor coverings. But these are finishing touches -- any carpentry, plumbing, or electrical work must be accomplished first. Older buildings, especially, may need new insulation, sheet rock, electrical wiring or fixtures, heating or air conditioning systems, copper pipes or other plumbing, or window and sash replacements.

In many areas, owners of large buildings furnish drapes, primarily to control the outside appearance of the building. In any case, some window coverings -- shades, drapes, or blinds -- should be hung and kept closed because obviously vacant apartments invite vandals and squatters. One owner hangs shades and traverse rods in his apartment building, then residents hang their own drapes. This individual installs rods rather than letting renters put up their own because the repeated installation and removal of rods by successive tenants damages the walls and woodwork.

Owners should consider the type of renter the building's floor plan and location will attract, then decorate the interior to appeal to that market. For example, a building situated in a rustic hillside neighborhood might feature hardwood floors, wooden beams, and earth colors.

Tenant Improvements:

Experienced building owners urge beginners to be cautious about permitting tenant improvements and to stipulate in the lease or rental agreement that *any* changes -- even painting -- must be approved in writing. Otherwise, renters may wreak some damages on units in the "improvement," like the couple who opted to paint their walls black. "You have no idea how many coats of paint it takes to cover black walls," groans the hapless owner.

Also, if the resident wants to install cupboards, bookcases, flower boxes, or room dividers, the property owner should make certain that they are property attached and cannot be easily dislodged. If such objects fall and injure a resident or visitor, the building owner might be liable. Any permanent improvements should remain at the end of tenancy.

Licenses:

City and county licensing requirements for rental property owners vary widely. In some areas owners of *any* type of rental property must obtain an annual business license; in other places, only owners of three or more units located on the same property need be licenses; and in at least one instance no business license need be obtained, but any rental property owner with annual gross receipts in excess of $4,000 must pay a city business tax. The minimum annual tax levied is $18.75 a year for owners earning up to $15,000 in gross rental receipts.

Property owners should contact their city anc county licensing agencies to learn the requirements in their areas.

In addition, rental property owners who are doing business under a name that varies from the corporate name, does not include the surnames of all owners, or implies the existence of additional owners must register this fictitious trade name with the county clerk within 40 days of beginning operation. The registration fee is $10. Within 30 days of this registration, notice of the fictitious trade name must be published in a general circulation newspaper in the county where the property is located. Publication costs average about #30. An affidavit affirming such publication must be filed within the next 30 days at the county clerk's office.

Setting Rents:

Almost all property owners want their rental income to at least cover expenses and mortgage payments; most want to make a profit as well. But many are unsure of exactly how much they can or should ask for rent.

One candid owner admits that he charges "whatever the market will bear. I ask the highest amount or even slightly higher than I think I can get. Then, if it seems to scare candidates off, I settle for a slightly lower rent.

As one professional manager stresses, "Supply and demand determine rental rates, regardless of a building's cost. In a tight market rents will rise until they match house payments. At that point, renters may become home seekers."

To set competitive rental rates, many owners frequently check the classified ads and often comparison shop similar units in nearby locations by posing as prospective residents. An owner who belongs to a local apartment association can ask other members what they charge for various sizes of units in several types of complexes or buildings with varying facilities.

ADVERTISING

Every day an apartment is vacant costs the owner money. To keep units filled, building owners and managers rely on several major advertising methods.

Signs:

Some apartment owners keep their property rented merely by posting inexpensive "For Rent" signs in windows. However, experts recommend the use of a simple but professionally painted sign which can be used repeatedly. "A clean-looking sign indicates a clean operation," contends one owner. And the reverse can also be true.

Signs can be adequate rental advertisement in a tight rental market, yet even those buildings located on busy boulevards may need more than signs since prospects would be limited to passersby. Thus, advertisers may prefer to combine signs with classified newspaper ads.

Newspaper Classified Ads:

Many property owners agree with the real estate tycoon who wrote, "the most dependable medium is a properly worded classified newspaper ad, short and to the point."

Well-written classified ads contain six elements:

1.   **Price** per month. Many newspapers list price first and/or categorize ads by rent levels.

2.   **Descriptive terms** such as "spacious," "luxurious," "modern," "sunny," "new," "quaint," "redecorated," or "secluded."

3.   **Location,** if not by street address, then at least indicating the general area such as "Glen Park district," "near downtown," or "three blocks from beach."

4.   **Number of rooms,** either the total number of rooms (excluding bathrooms) or the number of bedrooms. Ads may also mention if there is a separate dining room, den, breakfast nook, or more than one bath.

5.   **Telephone number** of the owner, manager, or agent.

6.   **Other essential details,** such as furnishings, utilities paid, or pets excluded, and any selling points like a yard, pool, playground, patio, garage, fireplace, laundry facility, or air conditioning.

One owner believes advertising should include some description — such as "working couple" or "young family" — indicating the type of tenant suitable to the dwelling or similar to current residents.

The shorter the classified ad, the less costly. Using abbreviations helps keep down ad costs, but shouldn't be overdone. An ad starting "rms riv vu" would not be understood by all apartment hunters.

If advertising costs in a major metropolitan daily seem too expensive, the small building owner might experiment with placing ads in smaller weekly newspapers in the same city. The owner of suburban units would probably advertise in the local rather than a city newspaper for the metropolitan area.

Apartment Locator Services/Brokers:

Some property owners prefer to turn the renting of vacant apartments over to real estate brokers or commercial apartment locator service firms who place advertisements, handle responses, and even check applicants' references. Typically, the cost for such a service may be 40% to 50% of one month's rent or 5% to 6% of the total lease.

Other Advertising Methods:

Referrals from satisfied renters can be one of the best ways of filling vacancies. A friendly, cooperative apartment manager can make each resident a salesperson for that building. Often a departing tenant will make a special effort to find a replacement. In fact, one landlord insists that the manager of a building whose residents don't like their dwelling well enough to recommend it to friends will have problems finding and keeping new renters.

SCREENING TENANTS

"A bad tenant is much worse than a vacant apartment," contends one Marin County broker. Most professionals agree that property owners should be discerning about whom they allow to rent their dwellings. Monetary losses caused by troublesome renters can be far greater than those incurred by letting an apartment stand empty while waiting for the right occupant.

Screening apartment seekers, both on the telephone and when showing the unit, helps weed out obviously unsuitable prospects. For example, a family owning three cars and a boat would not be good candidates for a building that has limited garage and parking space, and a couple with two sheepdogs would not be welcome in a condominium that has a "no pets" policy.

The manager of one 10-unit building where all the residents were youthful - and the walls paper-thin -- candidly told all callers that the units weren't soundproof, the driveway was steep, and the building had a lot of stairs.

Owners must remember that federal law prohibits discrimination on the basis of race, religion, sex, or national origin. California and local laws also prohibit certain other types of housing discrimination. The new building owner should be aware of all applicable federal, state, and local laws.

Some owners who have tried to subtly circumvent antidiscrimination laws by telling the apartment seeker that the dwelling was already rented or by asking for a higher rent or security deposit than previously specified have had their techniques backfire. Indeed, the rejected tenant can file a complaint with various federal and state agencies or sue in federal or state court. but property owners can still be selective on the basis of an applicant's appearance, attitude, income, family size, and pets.

Such selection may not only be legal, but economically essential. When showing a unit to prospects, a property owner should use the opportunity to not only sell the apartment but also size up the candidate. "I often rent by the feeling I get from people," claims one owner. "A couple of times I've been wrong, but not many." One San Francisco property owner points out to parents of small children that his apartments lack yards or play areas and are located on a busy boulevard, which might make them less desirable for families.

However, owners should not depend on personal impressions *alone*. Each prospective resident should fill out an application form, which may include all or some of the following information:

1.   Name of applicant and number of children who will reside in the apartment.

2.   Birthdate -- to make certain that applicants are old enough to legally sign a contract.

3.   Driver's license number -- a valuable way to trace a tenant who might later skip.

4.   Social Security Number.

5.   Name, address, and telephone number of person to be contacted in an emergency.

6.   Previous place of residence -- with length of time at that address as well as owner's or manager's name and phone number.

7.   Place of (current and/or previous) employment -- plus level of income, length of time on the job, superior's name and telephone number.

8.   Checking and/or savings account number(s).

9.   Current or terminated loan or charge account numbers.

10.   Vehicle registration number(s), make, model, year, color, and license plate number(s) for all cars, trucks, motorcycles, scooters, etc. (whether leased or owned).

11.   Consent for investigative consumer credit report.

Once this form has been completed, it should be scrutinized and the information checked, particularly employment information and past residences. One owner found that a prospect had lied when she said she was a teacher with the local school system. The school system had never heard of her. "False information on the application tells you that this person can't be trusted -- and probably won't pay the rent," reasons an experienced operator.

When calling an applicant's employer or landlord, another veteran property owner offers this tip: "Make sure the number you're calling *is* the guy's boss and not his best friend. Sometimes they try to set you up."

LEASES AND RENTAL AGREEMENTS

Most property owners negotiate either a month-to-month or a one-year rental agreement or lease with tenants.

A **month-to-month lease** runs for one month and is automatically renewed for one month at the end of each month. Most month-to-month contracts require the owner to give 30 days notice to raise the rent or to terminate the tenancy and tenants to give 30 days notice before vacating. Such agreements are common throughout California.

A **one-year (or longer) lease** or agreement fixes the rental rate for a longer period, the term of the lease. During this time the owner can plan on receiving agreed-upon rent but cannot increase the monthly amount or easily evict the tenant unless the terms of the lease are broken.

While all short and long-term leases and rental agreements are written documents, sometimes property owners enter into oral rental agreements with tenants. Such oral contracts may be legally binding but are not advisable.

"A proper lease/rental agreement may be the most important operating form and requires frequent updating," stresses one professional manager. While standard lease/agreement forms can be purchased at stationery or office supply stores, professionals strongly recommend the use of apartment or broker association copyrighted forms, which reflect current regulations. The owner who makes up an individual lease or agreement should have it checked by an attorney.

Security Deposits:

The typical deposit requested from tenants is a refundable sum of money -- called a security deposit -- to ensure that the rent is paid and that the premises are left in satisfactory condition when tenants vacate.

Security deposit amounts vary according to monthly rates; usually, the higher the rent, the higher the deposit, with average deposits of about $100 to $200. However, property experts warn owners to make deposits a **different amount from rent,** so tenants won't assume they are paying the last month's rent. For a $210-a-month apartment, for example, a property owner might ask a security deposit of $250.

In some areas tenants with young children may be required to pay a higher damage deposit. In other places, such requirements are illegal.

Security Deposit Insurance:

Security deposits often become a hotly disputed issue between building owners and tenants. Now, under a new plan launched by an innovative insurance firm, such friction can be eliminated.

Under the plan, the renter can use his or her personal credit rating to purchase credit insurance instead of paying the usual $100 to $200 cash deposit. The insurance costs the tenant 20% of the normal security deposit (up to twice the month's rental) and guarantees the tenant credit for the full amount of the deposit. In addition, the prospective tenant pays the firm a $10 fee for checking credit references.

However, if an insured resident leaves still owing rent or expenses for damages, the insurance company pays the building owner and then goes after the tenant to collect that loss. Apartment owners negotiate a master insurance contract with the insurance firm, indemnifying them for future losses resulting from uncollectible tenant debts. Owners pay a one-time administrative charge based on the number of units involved.

Pet Deposits:

Many buildings ban pets of all types. One landlady is adamant: "When I found that my tenants had a dog, I told them either the dog went, or they went."

However, as a property management professional points out, "At least 60% of the nation's households own one or more pets so apartment owners who ban animals from their buildings entirely cut off a sizable portion of the rental market." He advises owners to to prohibit pets, but to learn to control them and adds, "Then you'll get your share of all those pet owners who rent."

RAISING RENTS

Many owners dread raising rents because they fear an ensuing uproar from residents and a flurry of move-outs. Tenants naturally dislike paying more dollars for the same dwelling, and some will move out. But rising prices are a fact of life for property owners as well as renters. Just as rates for taxes and utilities go up, so rents escalate.

Collecting Rents:

Prompt collection of rents is vital to the successful operation of income property. If tenants don't pay, a small property owner will have trouble making payments on the mortgage loan or meeting other expenses. An owner operating on a narrow margin can lose the property in only a few months because of lost or late rents.

Careful selection of tenants is the first step toward steady rent collections. But even well-meaning residents may be tempted to let the rent slide if an owner is lax. Experts recommend that a firm policiy toward rental paymnets be instituted and that this policy be made very clear to tenants *before* they move in. Every new resident should understand the amount of the monthly payment, when it is due, and how it should be paid. Some owners require renters to pay both first and last months' rent before moving in. "Don't let anyone move in until they've paid at least the first month's rent and any deposits," cautions one victimized manager. "If they give you alibies in the beginning, you'll just get more of the same later." This landlord was persuaded to accept partial payment by a smooth-talking tenant who claimed he would pay athe remainder just as soon as his paycheck arrived. Later, the owner discovered numerous other creditors also waiting for their shares of that same paycheck. Eviction procedures were finally necessary to get rid of this nonpayer.

Manager Selection:

The manager of any apartment building or complex plalys a very important role in its success. Care must be taken to hire a person who will attract and kep desirable residents. "The manager sets the tone of the building and determines the caliber of tenants you get," emphasizes an owner. "A bad one poisons the whole atmosphere."

Some owners hire building residents as managers. Others advertise int he newspaper, use employment services, or hire experienced managers who are known to be seeking a change. Whatever the source, the individual hired should have a responsible, professional attitude toward the job. Skills needed will depend on the size of the complex and the tasks to be assigned by the owner. Most managers need at least minor maintenance skills, some recordkeeping ability, and a tactful, pleasant manner of dealing with people.

Instand of hiring experienced managers, one large property management firm concentrates on seeking out people in service-oriented jobs who appear able to carry out the owner's policies in a firm -- but friendly -- way.

Small property owners might do well to emulate the training programs of larger property management firmms and pay all or part of the costs for managers to enrollin appropriate courses at local colleges or universities. Local associations offer management courses. Also three national certification programs consisting of on-the-job experience and clasroom training exist for managers: The National Association of Home Builders' Registered Apartment Manager (RAM) program; and the Institute of Real Estate Management's Accredited Resident manager (ARM) program. Program courses cover such areas as human relations, salesmanship, supervision, maintenance, bookkeeping, purchasing, insurance, and budgeting.

Courses of study vary in length. For example the continuous CAM program in San Jose, offered by the Tri-County Apartment Association, is based on a five-week co urse given three times a year plus a series of seminars held over a two-year period. The ARM program is comprised of two to six-day seminars held in various areas several times a year.

Other Employees:

Aside from managers, at one time or another most small property owners need help in cleaning up apartments, making repairs, and performing other duties. According to the president of a Southern California property management company, the best approach is to hire a bonded independent contractor who carries a business license, decleares and contributes personal wage deductions, assumes legal liability, and carries appropriate insurance, including Worker's Compensation.

But if unskilled or casual labor is hired, the owner must be certain to comply with minimum wage laws. Also, time sheets and employee records should be kept, wage deductions made, and Workers' Compensation insurance carried.

BUILDING SECURITY

While making a building completely fire or crime-proof is impossible, certain devices can help protect the owner's investments and in some cases are required by local ordinance.

- **Smoke detection alarms** attached above bedroom doors alert the tenants to a fire and thus minimize both injury to tenants and damage to the owner's property.

- **Sprinkler systems** installed on ceilings help douse flames once a fire has started. Most commercial buildings have such sprinklers. Some owners install them in apartment buildings as well.

- **Peepscopes** permit residents to see who is outside their units without opening apartment doors.

- **Dead bolt locks** on doors make unauthorized entry more difficult. In some communities, ordinances require landlords to install such locks.

- **Window locks and grills** can be effective, but must not block fire exits.

- **Adequate lighting** in parking areas, garages, walkways, stairwells, and corridors helps deter burglars and vandals, who prefer to work in darkness.

- **Fire extinguishers** (governed by state laws regarding installation and accessibility) are only useful if tenants have been instructed in their use.

One property management consultant urges apartment owners not to hire 24-hour security patrols or canine patrols or to advertise a building security system. Pointing out that no apartment complex can be 100% secure, this expert contends that by publicizing security, the building owner assumes additional liability if a tenant is robbed, injured, or killed.

INSURANCE

Property owners who want to sleep well at night, knowing that investments are safe, protect their buildings by purchasing adequate insurance and reviewing coverage at least annually. Basic building coverage should include the following policies:

1. **Fire** and extended coverage reimbursing the owner for damage due to wind, hail, lightning, collapse, explosion, riots, smoke, or flood.

2. **Crime** insurance covering damage to the property arising from robbery, burglary, vandalism, malicious mischief, or employee theft.

3. **Liability** coverage protecting the owner against claims for accidents occurring on the property.

4. **Rent loss** insurance providing continuing rental income when apartments are rendered uninhabitable by a fire or other mishap.

5. **Workers' Compensation Insurance**, mandatory under California law, reimbursing disabled employees for medical expenses and lost wages due to injuries sustained on the job.

All of the above policies except Worker's Compensation can be purchases in an umbrella, multi peril policy, package for apartment houses. Such packages often offer significant savings over the same protection bought separately.

In addition to basic insurance listed above, the building owner may wish to purchase specialized insurance covering plate glass breakage, sprinkler leakage, earthquake damage, or boiler damage.

Also, fidelity bonds placed on individual employees who handle money protect owners against embezzlement. One experienced property owner suggests that owners purchase the highest liability limits obtainable on personal assets, because a property owner's assets often look very attractive to someone contemplating a lawsuit.

EVICTIONS/TERMINATIONS

At one time or another most property owners are faced with evicting a tenant from the premises. The usual reasons for eviction are nonpayment of rent, failure to abide by some part of the rental agreement -- keeping a dog when pets are prohibited or playing loud music that disturbs other tenants -- or refusal to leave after having been served a notice to vacate. Under California law the landlord of a month-to-month tenant can (except in certain circumstances) at any time, send a 30-day notice to leave for any reason.

To legally evict a tenant, a building owner must follow a very strict legal procedure, possibly resulting in a lawsuit in Small Claims or Municipal Court. If the owner wins the lawsuit and the tenant does not appeal to Superior Court, the sheriff or marshal then will evict the tenant after a nominal amount of time, granted by the court, for moving out voluntarily.

Because eviction proceedings are complicated and time-consuming, and because paperwork must be technically correct, many owners consult an attorney. Other property owners save money by handling the eviction themselves. Books are available which can guide a property owner who wishes to evict a resident without the help of an attorney. Notices and unlawful detainer forms can usually be obtained from local apartment associations.

Under no circumstances should a property owner harass, threaten, or use force to try to get rid of an obstreperous tenant. In addition, it is illegal for an owner to cut off utility service or otherwise make the dwelling uninhabitable, or to lock out the tenant and/or confiscate the tenant's belongings. Such illegal actions can result in a tenant's bringing legal action and being awarded money damages.

Appendix D

INSURANCE CHECKLIST

TYPE OF INSURANCE	PURCHASE	DO NOT PURCHASE
PROPERTY INSURANCE:		
Fire	_____	_____
Windstorm	_____	_____
Hail	_____	_____
Smoke	_____	_____
Explosion	_____	_____
Vandalism	_____	_____
Water Damage	_____	_____
Glass	_____	_____
LIABILITY INSURANCE	_____	_____
WORKERS' COMPENSATION	_____	_____
BUSINESS INTERRUPTION	_____	_____
DISHONESTY:		
Fidelity	_____	_____
Robbery	_____	_____
Burglary	_____	_____
Comprehensive	_____	_____
PERSONAL:		
Health	_____	_____
Life	_____	_____
Key Personnel	_____	_____

Special Appendix

Web Site Marketing

Business Web Site
an
Effective Marketing Tool

More than 100 million people use the Internet each day. A website offers help in marketing your small business. Your web site can help level the playing field for small businesses who compete with big businesses. It can enable small business to expand their business nationally or internationally.

What makes a good web site?

A good web site shows by doing; it proves rather than states. Instead of making claims, it provides evidence.

Evidence can take several forms:

- Case Studies showing how your efforts solved a previous client's problems.

- Testimonials from satisfied clients.

- Reprints of articles you've written or reviews of your work.

Education, however, remains the best way to establish credibility. To the extent prospects leave your web site better informed about your product or service, the easier it is to gain their respect (and their purchase order).

Three steps to creating your own business web site.

Today's tools make web publishing accessible to small businesses without programming experience. For example, Microsoft® Publisher 97 includes PageWizard design assistants, web deign elements and design checkers to help your build a workable web site.

Step one:

Choose a structure and a look. Your site should be structured and designed to best tell your story. But where do you start? Using the Page Wizard, you can choose from pre-designed options that can later be customized so that establishing a structure and "look" is easy.

Step two:

Tell your story. Next, simply select the sample headlines and text provided and replace them with words that describe what you have to offer.

Step three:

Check your work and post your site. The design in Publisher 97 goes through your web site element by element, identifying potential problems. Then, the web publishing wizard guides you through the process of posting your web site on the local Internet service provider or on-line service of your choice.

Remember, with millions of web sites, you may have to market your web site as well as your small business to get traffic for your business. The web site can be an inexpensive way of effectively building your small business.

10 tips for Web Site Online Marketing

1. Put up a simple web page.
2. Use a name that will attract people
3. Give away advice and information
4. Have lots of e-mail correspondence
5. Provide customized pages for users.
6. Visit user groups
7. Get on mailing lists
8. Arrange links with related sites
9. Make sure you're in every possible directory
10. Do not "SPAM"

INDEX

Step-by-Step Guides To Start, Manage & Market Your Own Business

4th Printing!

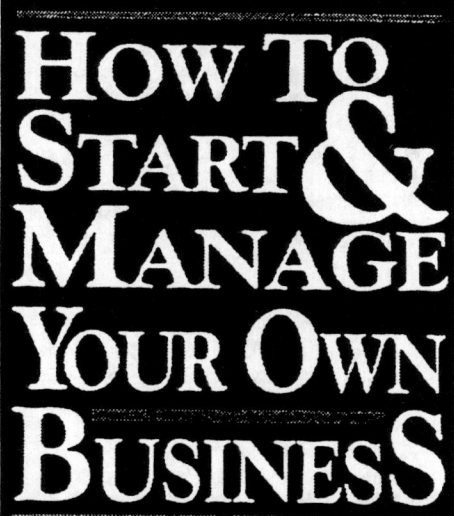

How To Start & Manage Your Own Business

For anyone who is looking to start-up a new business, this *step-by-step guide* includes planning, managing, marketing and promotion. **$18.95**

Soft Cover • 104 Pages
5 1/2" x 8 1/2" 0-9628759-0-2 ©1992

New!

How to Start & Manage a Home Based Business

This book provides the knowledge and tools necessary to successfully plan, design, and start up a new business in a practical way. With a step-by-step guide for planning, managing, marketing and promotion of a small business, in an easy-to-read and easy-to-understand format. The guidelines presented will help you pursue dreams of independence and financial success. **$18.95**

Soft Cover • 135 Pages
5 1/2" x 8 1/2" 1-887005-11-0 © 1996

3rd Printing!

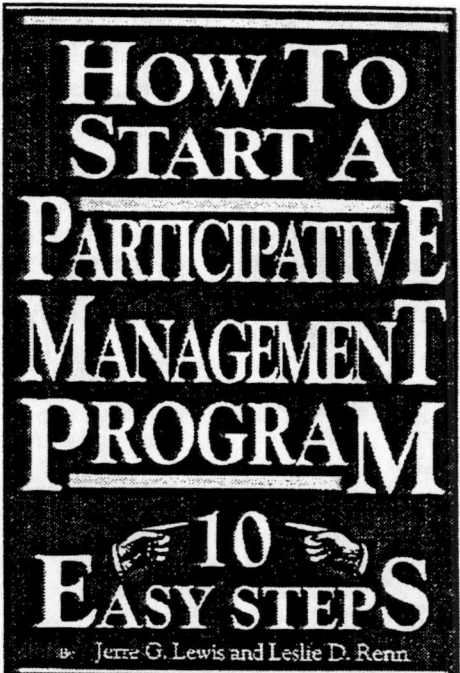

How To Start A Participative Management Program

A concise guide for small to midsize companies that is easy to read and follow *Step-by-step planning, managing and marketing of a small business* • How to empower and involve employees • Contains tools for measuring employees work environment. **$18.95**

Soft Cover • 93 Pages •
5 1/2" x 8 1/2", 0-9628759 ©1992

ABOUT THE AUTHORS

Jerre G. Lewis and Leslie D. Renn are both experienced professionals concerning small business management and entrepreneurship. For more than twenty years Mr. Lewis has been involved with business education at college level and the development of a series of small business seminars. He is a Certified Education Specialist for the U.S. Small Business Administration Volunteer Counseling Program. Mr. Renn is a business owner, entrepreneur, a small business consultant, and like Mr. Lewis, is involved with college level management instruction & business seminars. He also has extensive experience in large industry administration. Mr. Lewis and Mr. Renn received bachelors and masters degrees from Michigan universities, and both work and live in northern Michigan.

Business Books

Telephone 1-616-275-7287 • 1-517-684-1184 • Fax 1-517-684-3072

How to Start and Manage:

ISBN 1-57916-000-X An Apparel Store Business
ISBN 1-57916-001-8 A Word Processing Service Business
ISBN 1-57916-002-6 A Garden Center Business
ISBN 1-57916-003-4 A Hair Styling Shop Business
ISBN 1-57916-004-2 A Bicycle Shop Business
ISBN 1-57916-005-0 A Travel Agency Business
ISBN 1-57916-006-9 An Answering Service Business
ISBN 1-57916-007-7 A Health Spa Business
ISBN 1-57916-008-5 A Restaurant Business
ISBN 1-57916-009-3 A Specialty Food Store Business
ISBN 1-57916-010-7 A Welding Business
ISBN 1-57916-011-5 A Day Care Center Business
ISBN 1-57916-012-3 A Flower and Plant Store Business
ISBN 1-57916-013-1 A Construction Electrician Business
ISBN 1-57916-014-X A Housecleaning Service Business
ISBN 1-57916-015-8 A Nursing Service Business
ISBN 1-57916-016-6 A Bookkeeping Service Business
ISBN 1-57916-017-4 A Secretarial Service Business
ISBN 1-57916-018-2 A Bed and Breakfast Business
ISBN 1-57916-019-0 An Energy Specialist Business
ISBN 1-57916-020-4 A Guard Service Business
ISBN 1-57916-021-2 A Software Design Business
ISBN 1-57916-022-0 An Air Conditioning & Heating Business
ISBN 1-57916-023-9 A Plumbing Service Business
ISBN 1-57916-024-7 A Sewing Service Business
ISBN 1-57916-025-5 A Carpentry Service Business
ISBN 1-57916-026-3 A Home Attendent Service Business
ISBN 1-57916-027-1 A Tree Service Business
ISBN 1-57916-028-X A Dairy Farming Business
ISBN 1-57916-029-8 A Farm Equipment Repair Service Business
ISBN 1-57916-030-1 A Children's Clothing Store Business
ISBN 1-57916-031-X A Women's Apparel Store
ISBN 1-57916-032-8 A Convenience Food Store Business
ISBN 1-57916-033-6 A Pest Control Service Business
ISBN 1-57916-034-4 A Printing Business
ISBN 1-57916-035-2 An Ice Cream Business
ISBN 1-57916-036-0 A Mail Order Business
ISBN 1-57916-037-9 A Bookstore Business
ISBN 1-57916-038-7 A Home Furnishing Business
ISBN 1-57916-039-5 A Retail Florist Business
ISBN 1-57916-040-9 A Radio-Television Repair Shop Business
ISBN 1-57916-041-7 A Dry Cleaning Business
ISBN 1-57916-042-5 A Hardware Store Business
ISBN 1-57916-043-3 A Marine Retailing Business
ISBN 1-57916-044-1 An Office Products Business
ISBN 1-57916-045-X A Pharmacy Business
ISBN 1-57916-046-8 A Fish Farming Business
ISBN 1-57916-047-6 A Personal Referral Service Business
ISBN 1-57916-048-4 A Solar Energy Business
ISBN 1-57916-049-2 A Building Service Contracting Business
ISBN 1-57916-050-6 A Retail Decorating Products Business
ISBN 1-57916-051-4 A Sporting Goods Store Business
ISBN 1-57916-052-2 A Retail Grocery Store
ISBN 1-57916-053-0 A Cosmetology Business
ISBN 1-57916-054-9 A Franchised Business
ISBN 1-57916-055-7 An Electronics Industry Consulting Practice Business
ISBN 1-57916-056-5 An Independent Consulting Practice Business
ISBN 1-57916-057-3 An Independent Trucking Business
ISBN 1-57916-058-1 An Accounting Service Business

ISBN 1-57916-059-X A Nursery Business
ISBN 1-57916-060-3 A Seminar Promotion Business
ISBN 1-57916-061-1 A Bar & Cocktail Lounge Business
ISBN 1-57916-062-X A Wheelchair Transportation Business
ISBN 1-57916-063-8 A Fertilizer and Pesticide Business
ISBN 1-57916-064-6 A Desktop Publishing Business
ISBN 1-57916-065-4 A Crime Prevention Business
ISBN 1-57916-066-2 A Gift Shop Business
ISBN 1-57916-067-0 A Handcraft Success Business
ISBN 1-57916-068-9 A Coin-Operated Laundries Business
ISBN 1-57916-069-7 A Property Management Business
ISBN 1-57916-070-0 An Auto Supply Store Business
ISBN 1-57916-071-9 A Men's Apparel Store Business
ISBN 1-57916-072-7 A Temporary Help Service Business
ISBN 1-57916-073-5 An Advertising Agency Business
ISBN 1-57916-074-3 A Firewood Sales Business
ISBN 1-57916-075-1 A Children's Bookstore Business
ISBN 1-57916-076-X A Used Bookstore Business
ISBN 1-57916-077-8 A Sandwich Shop Deli Business
ISBN 1-57916-078-6 An Instant Print/Copy Shop
ISBN 1-57916-079-4 A Gift Specialty Store Business
ISBN 1-57916-080-8 A Gift Basket Service Business
ISBN 1-57916-081-6 A Hospitality Management Business
ISBN 1-57916-082-4 A Hotel Business
ISBN 1-57916-083-2 A Catering Service Business
ISBN 1-57916-084-0 A Carpet-Cleaning Service Business
ISBN 1-57916-085-9 A Window-Washing Service Business
ISBN 1-57916-086-7 An Innkeeping Service Business
ISBN 1-57916-087-5 An Apartment Preparation Service
ISBN 1-57916-088-3 A Kiosks and Cart Business
ISBN 1-57916-089-1 A Janitorial Service Business
ISBN 1-57916-090-5 A Medical Claims Processing Business
ISBN 1-57916-091-3 A Nursing Home Care Business
ISBN 1-57916-092-1 A Home Health Care Business
ISBN 1-57916-093-X A Referral Services Business
ISBN 1-57916-094-8 A Hair Styling Salon Business
ISBN 1-57916-095-6 A Child Care Service Business

How-To Business Books

ISBN 1-57916-096-4 How to Buy and Sell A Business
ISBN 1-57916-097-2 How to Advertise A Small Business
ISBN 1-57916-098-0 How to Write A Successful Business Plan
ISBN 1-57916-099-9 How to Finance Your Business for the 21st Century
ISBN 1-57916-100-6 How to Market Your Business for the 21st Century

Library Discount - 20%
Retail Discount - 20%
$3.00 Postage & Handling
$18.95 Each

To Order Business Plans

Please Remit To:
    Lewis & Renn Associates
    10315 Harmony Drive
    Interlochen, Michigan 49643

Business Book # 1-57916-_____ Title _____

Business Book # 1-57916-_____ Title _____

Name _____

Address _____

City _____

State_____ Zip _____

Business Book _____

U.S. Shipping & Postage $ 3.00

Total _____